ISLAM & SECULARISM

SYED MUHAMMAD NAQUIB AL-ATTAS

Qadeem
PRESS

ISLAM & SECULARISM

SYED MUHAMMAD
NAQUIB AL-ATTAS

M.A (McGill), Ph.D (london)
University Professor of Islamic Thought and
Civilization: Founder Director
International Institute of Islamic Thought and
Civilization: First Holder of the Distinguished
al-Ghazali Chair of Islamic Thought

Qadeem Press Edition
Breathing Life into Forgotten Pages
www.qadeempress.com

Original Edition Published by ISTAC, IIUM, Malaysia

Find our titles on your favourite online bookstore using the keyword 'Qadeem Press'

TO

THE MUSLIM YOUTH

CONTENTS

List of Figures

AUTHOR'S NOTE
TO THE FIRST EDITION

The present book is a development of ideas contained in the many paragraphs of another book in Malay entitled: *Risalah Untuk Kaum Muslimin,* which I wrote and completed during the first few months of 1974. Due to many circumstances which demanded my attention at home and abroad, however, the *Risalah* has not yet been sent to the press.

In this book, what is contained in Chapter III was composed and completed during the month of Ramaḍān of 1395 (1975), and delivered as a Lecture under the same title to the International Islamic Conference held in April 1976 at the Royal Commonwealth Society, London, in conjunction with the World of Islam Festival celebrated there that year. It was published as a monograph in the same year by the Muslim Youth Movement of Malaysia (ABIM), Kuala Lumpur, and in 1978 it appeared, together with other Lectures delivered on the same occasion by various Muslim scholars, in a book of one volume entitled: *The Challenge of Islam,* edited by Altaf Gauhar and published by the Islamic Council of Europe, London.

All the other Chapters of the book were begun in March 1977 and completed in April of the same year, during my appointment as Visiting Scholar and Professor of Islamics at the Department of Religion, Temple University, Philadelphia, U.S.A., in the Winter and Spring of 1976–1977. What is contained in Chapter V was presented as a Paper entitled: "Preliminary Thoughts on the Nature of Knowledge and the Definition and Aims of Education", addressed to the First World Conference on Muslim Education held at Mecca in April 1977. It will appear, together with other selected Papers of the Conference, in a book entitled: *Aims and Objectives of Islamic Education,* edited with an introduction by myself and published by King Abdulaziz University and Hodder & Stoughton, London, 1979, as one of a series of seven books.

Syed Muhammad Naquib al-Attas
Kuala Lumpur, Muḥarram 1399/December 1978.

PREFACE TO THE SECOND PRINTING

Almost twenty years have elapsed since the first printing of this book, but the seminal ideas pertaining to the problem of Muslim education and allied topics of an intellectual and revolutionary nature, such as the idea of islamization of contemporary knowledge and a general definition of its nature and method, and the idea of the Islamic University, the conceptualization of its nature and final establishment, were formulated much earlier in the mid-nineteen-sixties. They were formulated, elaborated, and disseminated here in Malaysia and abroad in academic lectures and various conferences and more than 400 public lectures, and were born out of the need for creative thinking and clarification of the basic concepts based upon the religious and intellectual tradition of Islām, and upon personal observation and reflection and conceptual analysis throughout my teaching experience in Malaysian universities since 1964. These ideas have also been communicated to the Islamic Secretariat in Jeddah in early 1973, at the same time urging the relevant authorities to convene a gathering of reputable scholars of Islām to discuss and deliberate upon them.[1] There is no doubt that these ideas have been instrumental in the convening of the First World Conference on Muslim Education held at Mekkah in early 1977, where the substance of Chapter V of this book was published in English and Arabic and read as a keynote address at the Plenary Session.[2] In 1980, a commentary of a few paragraphs of that Chapter pertaining to the concept of education in Islām was presented and read as a keynote address at the Plenary Session of the Second World Conference on Muslim

---

1 Document sent to the Secretariat dated 15 May 1973.
2 On April 3, 1977 (see the *Conference Book*, King Abdul Aziz University, Jeddah and Mecca al-Mukarramah, 1397/1977, pp. 35 and 37).

Education held at Islamabad early the same year.[3]

Thenceforth, for the successive convenings of the World Conference on Muslim Education held in various Muslim capital cities, I was not invited and my ideas have been appropriated without due acknowledgement and propagated since 1982 by ambitious scholars, activists, academic operators and journalists in vulgarized forms to the present day.[4] Muslims must be warned that plagiarists and pretenders as well as ignorant imitators affect great mischief by debasing values, imposing upon the ignorant, and encouraging the rise of mediocrity. They appropriate original ideas for hasty implementation and make false claims for themselves. Original ideas cannot be implemented when vulgarized; on the contrary, what is

---

3　See my *The Concept of Education in Islām,* Kuala Lumpur 1980, p.v. and note 2.

4　In January 1982 a seminar was held in Islamabad focussing its attention to and calling for the 'Islamization of Knowledge', a phrase which was taken from this very book (see p. 162). As mentioned above, Chapter V of this book was published in English and in Arabic, and presented and read as a keynote address in the First World Conference Muslim Education held at Mekkah in early 1977. The phrase is found on page 21 of the English version. Indeed, not merely the phrase, but the whole idea including the plan of what constitutes the islamization of knowledge and the method of its implementation, as well as the conceptualization of the Islamic university, came from this book (together with the commentary of a few paragraphs in Chapter V, i.e. the work entitled: *The Concept of Education in Islām,* 1980), whose contents were made known to Professor Ismail R. al-Faruqi since 1976. The manuscript of this book was entrusted to him for publication at that time, and I never saw it again. When it became apparent to me that he was betraying the trust I put in him concerning authorship of the seminal ideas contained in the book, and sensing his intention to make use of them himself, I subsequently had the book published here in Kuala Lumpur in 1078. There is no doubt that this book and the book elaborating on the concept of education in Islām have been appropriated by al-Faruqi for the convening of the seminar at Islamabad, to which I was obviously not welcomed and after which his *Islamization of Knowledge,* printed in Maryland, U.S.A. in 1982, appeared.

praiseworthy in them will turn out to become blameworthy, and their rejection will follow with the dissatisfaction that will emerge. So in this way authentic and creative intellectual effort will continually be sabotaged. It is not surprising that the situation arising out of the loss of *adab* also provides the breeding ground for the emergence of extremists who make ignorance their capital.

Since the value and validity of new ideas can best be developed and clarified along logical lines by their original source, I have by means of my own thought, initiative and creative effort, and with God's succour and the aid of those whom God has guided to render their support, conceived and established an international Institute aligned to the purpose of the further development, clarification and correct implementation of these ideas until they may come to full realization.

The International Institute of Islamic Thought and Civilization (ISTAC), although formulated and conceptualized much earlier, was officially opened in 1991, and among its most important aims and objectives are to conceptualize, clarify, elaborate, scientific and epistemological problems encountered by Muslims in the present age; to provide an Islamic response to the intellectual and cultural challenges of the modern world and various schools of thought, religion, and ideology; to formulate an Islamic philosophy of education, including the definition, aims and objectives of Islamic education; to formulate an Islamic philosophy of science; to study the meaning and philosophy of Islamic art and architecture, and to provide guidance for the islamization of the arts and art education; to publish the results of our researches and studies from time to time for dissemination in the Muslim World; to establish a superior library reflecting the religious and intellectual traditions both of the Islamic and Western civilizations as a means to attaining the realization of the above aims and objectives. Those with understanding and discernment will know, when they ponder over the significance of these aims and objectives, that these are not merely empty slogans, for they will realize that these aims and objectives reflect a profound grasp of the real problems confronting the contemporary Muslim world. The aims and objectives of the Institute are by no means easy to accomplish. But with concerted effort from dedicated and proven scholars who will deliberate as a sort of organic body which is itself rooted in authentic Islamic learning and are at the same time able to teach various modern disciplines, we shall, God willing, realize the fulfilment of our vision. Even so, a significant measure of these aims and objectives has in fact already been realized in various stages of fulfilment. Concise books have already been published by ISTAC outlining frameworks for Islamic philosophies of education including its definition and its aims and objectives;[5] of science;[6] of psychology and epistemology,[7] as well as other such works which altogether will be integrated to project what I believe to be the worldview of Islām.[8] It is within the framework of this worldview, formulated in terms of a metaphysics, that our philosophy of science and our sciences in general must find correspondence and coherence with truth. ISTAC has already begun operating as a graduate institution of higher learning open to international scholars and students engaged in research and studies on Islamic theology, philosophy, and metaphysics; science, civilization, languages and comparative thought and religion. It has

---

5 Al-Attas, *The Concept of Education in Islām*, ISTAC, Kuala Lumpur, 1991 (first published in 1980).

.6 *Ibid., Islām and the Philosophy of Science*, ISTAC, Kuala Lumpur, 1989.

7 *Ibid., The Nature of Man and the Psychology of the Human Soul*, ISTAC, Kuala Lumpur, 1990.

8 *Ibid., The Intuition of Existence*, ISTAC, Kuala Lumpur, 1990; *On Quiddity and Essence*, ISTAC, Kuala Lumpur, 1990; *The Meaning and Experience of Happiness in Islām*, ISTAC, Kuala Lumpur, 1993. These, together with the works cited in notes 6 and 7, represent outlines of Islamic psychology, cosmology and ontology forming the substance of a forthcoming book entitled *Prolegomena to the Metaphysics of Islām*.

already assembled a respectable and noble library reflecting the fields encompassing its aims and objectives; and the architecture of ISTAC is itself a concrete manifestation of artistic expression that springs from the well of creative knowledge.[9]

This book was originally dedicated to the emergent Muslims, for whose hearing and understanding it was indeed meant, in the hope that they would be intelligently prepared, when their time comes, to weather with discernment the pestilential winds of secularization and with courage to create necessary changes in the realm of our thinking that is still floundering in the sea of bewilderment and self-doubt. The secularizing 'values' and events that have been predicted would happen in the Muslim world have now begun to unfold with increasing momentum and persistence due still to the Muslims' lack of understanding of the true nature and implications of secularization as a philosophical program. It must be emphasized that our assault on secularism is not so much directed toward what is generally understood as 'secular' Muslim state and government, but more toward secularization as a philosophical program, which 'secular' Muslim states and governments need not necessarily have to adopt. The common understanding among Muslims, no doubt indoctrinated by Western notions, is that a secular state is a state that is not governed by the *'ulamā'*, or whose legal system is not established upon the revealed law. In other words it is not a theocratic state. But this setting in contrast the secular state with the theocratic state is not really an Islamic way of understanding the matter, for since Islām does not involve itself in the dichotomy between the sacred and the profane, how then can it set in contrast the theocratic state with the secular state? An Islamic state is neither wholly theocratic nor wholly secular. A Muslim

---

9 See the brief intellectual history and philosophy of ISTAC outlined in *The Beacon on the Crest of a Hill*, ISTAC, Kuala Lumpur, 1991, by Dr. Wan Mohd. Nor Wan Daud, who is Associate Professor at ISTAC.

state calling itself secular does not necessarily have to oppose religious truth and religious education; does not necessarily have to divest nature of spiritual meaning; does not necessarily have to deny religious values and virtues in politics and human affairs. But the philosophical and scientific process which I call 'secularization' necessarily involves the divesting of spiritual meaning from the world of nature; the desacralization of politics from human affairs; and the deconsecration of values from the human mind and conduct. Remember that we are a people neither accustomed nor permitted to lose hope and confidence, so that it is not possible for us simply to do nothing but wrangle among ourselves and rave about empty slogans and negative activism while letting the real challenge of the age engulf us without positive resistance. The real challenge is intellectual in nature, and the positive resistance must be mounted from the fortification not merely of political power, but of power that is founded upon right knowledge.

We are now again at the crossroads of history, and awareness of Islamic identity is beginning to dawn in the consciousness of emergent Muslims. Only when this awareness comes to full awakening with the sun of knowledge will there emerge from among us men and women of spiritual and intellectual maturity and integrity who will be able to play their role with wisdom and justice in upholding the truth. Such men and women will know that they must return to the early masters of the religious and intellectual tradition of Islām, which was established upon the sacred foundation of the Holy Qur'ān and the Tradition of the Holy Prophet, in order to learn from the past and be able to acquip spiritually and intellectually for the future; they will realize that they must not simply appropriate and imitate what modern secular Western civilization has created, but must regain by exerting their own creative knowledge, will, and imagination what is lost of the Muslims' purpose in life, their history, their values and virtues embodied in their sciences, for what is lost can

never be regained by blind imitation and the raving of
slogans which deafen with the din of 'development'; they
will discern that development must not involve a
correspondence of Islām with the facts of contemporary
events that have strayed far from the path of truth;[10] and
they will conceive and formulate their own definitions and
conceptions of government and of the nature of
development that will correspond with the purpose of
Islām. Their emergence is conditional not merely upon
physical struggle, but more upon the achievement of true
knowledge, confidence and boldness of vision that is able
to create great changes in history.

Syed Muhammad Naquib Al-Attas
Kuala Lumpur
27 Muḥarram 1414/17 July 1993

---

10 See my *Islām and the Philosophy of Science, op. cit.,* pp. 23-25.

بسم الله الرحمن الرحيم
الحمد لله رب العالمين
الصلاة والسلام على اشرف الأنبياءوالمرسلين

I

THE CONTEMPORARY WESTERN CHRISTIAN BACKGROUND

About ten years ago* the influential Christian philosopher and one regarded by Christians as among the foremost of this century, Jacques Maritain, described how Christianity and the Western world were going through a grave crisis brought about by contemporary events arising out of the experience and understanding and interpretation of life in the urban civilization as manifested in the trend of neo-modernist thought which emerged from among the Christians themselves and the intellectuals — philosophers, theologians, poets, novelists, writers, artists — who represent Western culture and civilization.[1] Since the European Enlightenment, stretching from the 17th to the 19th centuries, and with the concomitant rise of reason and empiricism and scientific and technological advances in the West, English, Dutch, French and German philosophers have indeed foreshadowed in their writings the crisis that Maritain described, though not quite in the same manner and dimension, for the latter was describing in conscious and penetrating perception the events of contemporary experience only known as an adumbrated prediction in the past. Some Christian theologians in the

---

* This was written in 1976.

1   See his *Le Paysan de la Garonne*, Paris, 1966.

earlier half of this century also foresaw the coming of such a crisis, which is called *secularization*. Already in the earlier half of the 19th century the French philosopher-sociologist, Auguste Comte, envisaged the rise of science and the over-throw of religion, and believed, according to the secular logic in the development of Western philosophy and science, that society was 'evolving' and 'developing' from the primitive to the modern stages, and observed that taken in its developmental aspect metaphysics is a tran-sition from theology to science;[2] and later that century the German philosopher-poet and visionary, Friedrich Nietzsche, prophesied through the mouth of Zarathustra—at least for the Western world — that God is dead.[3] Western philosophers, poets, novelists have anticipated its coming and hailed it as preparing for an 'emancipated' world with no 'God' and no 'religion' at all. The French Jesuit, pale-ontologist Pierre Tielhard de Chardin, followed by other theologians like the German Dietrich Bonhoeffer and the American Paul Tillich, sensing the trend of contemporary events and the thoughts that recognized their significance to Christianity and the Western world, began to accept the inevitability of the impending religious and theological crisis that would emerge as a result of secularization, and being already influenced by it they counselled alignment and participation in the process of secularization, which is seen by many as irresistably spreading rapidly throughout the world like a raging contagion.[4] The Nietzschean cry the

2   See his *General View of Positivism*, trans. J.H. Bridges, London, 1880. Also H. Martineau's *Comte's Positive Philosophy*, London, 1853.

3   See H.L. Mencken's the *Philosophy of Nietzsche*, Boston, 1913. For a brief but popular commentary on Nietzsche's philoso-phy, see W. Durant, *The Story of Philosophy*, New York, 1926, chapter IX. The Modern Library, New York, has published some of his works in one volume (The Philosophy of Nietzsche) containing *Zarathustra*, *Beyond Good and Evil*, *Genealogy of Morals*, *Ecce Homo*, and *Birth of Tragedy*.

4   For Tielhard de Chardin's thoughts, see his *The Future of*

'God is dead', which is still ringing in the Western world, is now mingled with the dirge that 'Christianity is dead'; and some of the influential theologians among the Christians — particularly the Protestants, who seem to accept the fate of traditional Christianity as such, and are more readily inclined toward changing with the times — have even started to initiate preparations for the laying out of a new theological ground above the wreckage in which lay the dissolute body of traditional Christianity, out of which a new secularized Christianity might be resurrected. These theologians and theorists align themselves with the forces of neo-modernist thought. They went so far as to assert triumphantly, in their desire to keep in line with contemporary events in the West, that secularization has its roots in biblical faith and is the fruit of the Gospel and, therefore, rather than oppose the secularizing process, Christianity must realistically welcome it as a process congenial to its true nature and purpose. European and American theologians and theorists like Karl Barth, Friedrich Gogarten, Rudolph Bultmann, Gerhard von Rad, Arend van Leeuwen, Paul van Buren, Harvey Cox and Leslie Dewart — and many more in Europe, England and America, both Catholic and Protestant — have found cause to call for radical changes in the interpretation of the Gospel and in the nature and role of the Church that would merge them logically and naturally into the picture of contemporary Western man and his world as envisaged in the secular panorama of life.[5] While some of the Christian theologians

---

Man, London, 1964; and *The Appearance of Man*, New York, 1966. For Bonhoeffer, see his *Ethics*, New York, 1955; and *Prisoner for God*, New York, 1959. For Tillich, see his *Systematic Theology*, Chicago, 1951 (vol. I); and *The Courage to Be*, New Haven, 1952.

5   For an expression of their ideas, see Barth, *Church Dogmatics*, Edinburgh 1956–1963; *The Humanity of God*, Richmond, Va., 1960; Gogarten, *Verhängnis und Hoffnung der Neuziet*, Stuttgart, 1953; *Der Mensch zwischen Gott und Welt*, Stuttgart, 1956;

and intellectuals think that the religious and theological crisis felt by them has not yet taken hold of the Christian community, others feel that the generality among them and not only the intellectuals are already enmeshed in the crisis. Its grave implications for the future of traditional Christianity is widely admitted, and many are beginning to believe in the predictions of the Austrian psychoanalyst, Sigmund Freud, whose *The Future of an Illusion*[6] is regarded as the greatest assault on theism in Western history. Furthermore the Christians who on the whole are apparently opposed to secularization, are themselves unconsciously assiduous accomplices in that very process, to the extent that those aware of the dilemma confronting them have raised general alarm in that there has now emerged with increasing numbers and persistence what Maritain has called "immanent apostasy" within the Christian community.[7] Indeed many Christian theologians and intellectuals forming the avant-garde of the Church are in fact deeply involved in 'immanent apostasy', for while firmly resolving to remain Christian at all costs they openly profess and advocate a secularized version of it, thus ushering into the Christian fold a new emergent Christianity alien to the traditional version to gradually change and supplant it from within. In such a state of affairs it is indeed not quite an exaggeration to say that we are perhaps spectators of events which may yet lead to another Reformation in Christian history.[8] The theologians and intellectuals referred to above are not only preparing

---

Bultmann, *Theology of the New Testament*, New York, 1951 (vol. I) and 1955 (vol. II); Von Rad, *Genesis: A Commentary*, Philadelphia, 1961; Van Buren, *The Secular Meaning of the Gospel*, New York, 1963; Van Leeuwen, *Christianity and World History*, New York, 1965; Cox, *The Secular City*, New York, 1965; Dewart, *The Future of Belief*, New York, 1966.

6   London, 1928.

7   *Le Paysan de la Garonne*, p. 16.

8   See John A.T. Robinson, *The New Reformation?*, London, 1965.

ground for a new secularized version of Christianity, but they also tragically know and accept as a matter of historical fact that the very ground itself will be ever-shifting, for they have come to realize, by the very relativistic nature of their new interpretation, that that new version itself — like all new versions to come — will ultimately again be replaced by another and another and so on, each giving way to the other as future social changes demand. They visualize the contemporary experience of secularization as part of the 'evolutionary' process of human history; as part of the irreversible process of 'coming of age', of 'growing up' to 'maturity' when they will have to 'put away childish things' and learn to have 'the courage to be'; as part of the *inevitable* process of social and political change and the corresponding change in values almost in line with the Marxian vision of human history. And so in their belief in permanent 'revolution' and permanent 'conversion' they echo within their existential experience and consciousness the confession of the Danish philosopher Sören Kierkegaard: "We are always becoming Christians".[9] Thus they naturally advocate in their attempt to align themselves with secularization a reconceptualization of the Christian Gospel; a redefinition of their concept of God; a dehellenization of Christian dogma. And Christianity, by virtue of its cultural nature and developmental experience, and based as it has always been upon a historically shifting foundation of hermeneutics, might lend itself easily to the possible realization of their vision of the future. This trend of events, disconcerting to many traditional Christians, is causing much anxiety and foreboding and reflected plainly in Mascall's book where he reiterates that instead of converting the world to Christianity they are converting Christianity to the world.[10]

While these portents of drastic change have aroused the

---

9 See his *The Present Age*, New York, 1962.

10 E.L. Mascall, *The Secularization of Christianity*, New York, 1966, *passim*, e.g., pp. 101–2.

consternation of the traditional Catholic theologians, whose appeals of distress have caused Pope John XXIII to call for an *aggiornamento* to study ways and means to overcome, or at least to contain, the revolutionary crisis in the Christian religion and theology, and to resist secularization through the enunciation of the ecumenical movement, and the initiation of meaningful dialogues with Muslims and others, in the hope not only of uniting the Christian community but of enlisting our conscious or unconscious support as well in exorcising the immanent enemy, they nonetheless admit, albeit grudgingly, that their theology as understood and interpreted during these last seven centuries is now indeed completely out of touch with the 'spirit of the times' and is in need of serious scrutiny as a prelude towards revision. The Protestants, initiated by the 19th century German theologian and historian of the development of Christian dogma, Adolf von Harnack, have since been pressing for the dehellenization of Christianity;[11] and today even Catholics are responding to this call, for now they all see that, according to them, it was the casting of Christianity in Hellenic forms in the early centuries of its development that is responsible, among other tenacious and perplexing problems, for the conceiving of God as a suprarational Person; for making possible the inextricably complicated doctrine of the Trinity; for creating the condition for the possibility of modern atheism in their midst — a possibility that has in fact been realized. This is a sore point for the Catholic theologians who cleave to the permanence of tradition, who realize that the discrediting of Hellenic epistemology — particularly with reference to the Parmenidean theory of truth, which formed the basis of Scholastic thought centered on the Thomistic metaphysics of Being — must necessarily involve Catholicism in a revolution of Christian theology. For this reason perhaps — that is, to meet the challenge of the Protestant onslaught which came with the

---

11 See his *History of Dogma*, (Eng. trans.), London, 1894–99.

tide of the inexorable advance of Modernist thought in the European Enlightenment, and the logical development of the epistemological theory and method of the French philosopher, René Descartes, which greatly influenced the form in which European philosophy and science was to take — renewed interest in the study of Thomistic metaphysics have gained momentum this century among Catholic philosophers such as Maritain, Etienne Gilson and Joseph Maréchal, who each has his own school of interpretation cast within the infallible metaphysical mould fashioned by the Angelic Doctor. But some of the disciples of the former two, notably Dewart[12] and his followers, while not going as far as Von Harnack in condemning hellenization as the perpetrator in the corruption of Christian dogma, nonetheless admit that hellenization has been responsible for retarding the development of Christian dogma, restricting its growth, as it were, to the playpen of philosophical enquiry and its development to the kindergarten of human thought. So in 'a world come of age', they argue controversially, Christian thought must no longer — cannot any longer — be confined to the crib of childish and infantile illusions if it were to be allowed to rise to the real challenge of maturity. And thus with new impetus derived from the phenomenology of Edmund Husserl and the existentialism of Martin Heidegger, and further fortified by recent advances in linguistic analyses contributed by the philosophers of language, notably those belonging to the Vienna Circle,[13] they press on vigorously for the

---

12　See Dewart's *The Future of Belief,* cited in note 5 above. The title of the book, also subtitled: *'Theism in a World Come of Age',* alludes to Freud's work cited in note 6 above. The subtitle alludes to a phrase of Bonhoeffer on the maturing of the consciousness of Western man.

13　The 'Vienna Circle' was the name invented and suggested by Otto Neurath for a group of renowned philosophers — of which he was a member — formed around the physicist-philosopher, Moritz Schlick, at the University of Vienna from

demythologization of Christian scripture and the dehellenization of its dogma.

Whatever the outcome may be Christians as a whole do not deny that their most serious problem is the 'problem of God'. Already as alluded to briefly in connection with the Parmenidean correspondence theory of truth, the problem of God is outlined against the background of the problem of the existence of objects. Since according to Parmenides thought and being are identical, and being is that which fills space, it follows that in the correspondence theory of truth a proposition or an uttered thought or meaning is true only if there is a fact to which it corresponds. Being as such is necessary. The later Greek philosophers including Plato and Aristotle never doubted the necessity of being. Indeed, to regard being as necessary was the essential element of the Greek world view. However they distinguished between the necessity of being as such — that is, as concrete reality, existing as actuality as a whole — and individual beings, regarding individual beings as contingent. The being of the world as such is necessary and hence also eternal, but individual beings, including that of a man, are contingent as they have an origination

---

1925–1936. They formulated what is known as 'the scientific conception of the world' characterized by two features: it is *empiricist* and *positivist*, and is marked by the application of a certain method, namely *logical analysis*, as practised in modern symbolic logic. Their secular, scientific world-conception influenced many branches of formal and empirical sciences extending beyond philosophy, such as arithmetic, physics, geometry, biology and psychology, and the social sciences. The leading representatives of the Circle's scientific world-conception were Albert Einstein, Bertrand Russell and Ludwig Wittgenstein. For a concise exposition of the historical background of the Vienna Circle, its scientific world-conception, its discussion of fields of problems, see Otto Neurath's *Empiricism and Sociology*, Dordrecht, 1973, X.

in time and space and suffer change and dissolution and final end. The being of man as a species, however, like the being of the world as such, is necessary and indeed also eternal. It is quite obvious that when Christianity officially adopted Aristotelian philosophy into its theology,[14] it had to deny necessary being to the creatures and affirm necessary being only to God Who alone is Eternal. Thus whereas Christian scholastic theology, like the Greeks, affirmed God as the Supreme Being Whose Being is Necessary, it did not regard the being of the world and nature as necessary, for as created being the world is by nature contingent. However, since it continued to adopt the Parmenidean epistemology, and while it denied necessary being to the creatures, it could not deny the necessity of the being of creatures as to their intelligibility; hence the creatures are contingent *as to their being,* but necessary *as to their being in thought.* In this way the identity of being — and also its necessity — and intelligibility is retained. Since a distinction was made between necessary being and contingent being, and with reference to the creatures their being necessary is in thought and not in actuality, a real distinction was thus made between *essence* and *existence* in creatures. The essence of the creature is its being in thought, and this is necessary; its existence is its actuality outside of thought, and this is contingent. As to God, it was affirmed that obviously His Essence should be identical with His Existence as Necessary Being. This distinction between essence and existence in creatures was apparently made on the basis of Thomas Aquinas' observation, which in turn seems to have been based on a misunderstanding of Avicenna's position, that every essence or quiddity can be understood without anything being known of its existing, and that, therefore, the act of existing is other than

---

14 *I.e.,* as accomplished by Thomas Aquinas in what came to be known as the Thomistic Synthesis, see further below, pp. 33–36.

essence or quiddity.[15] The only Being whose quiddity is also its very act of existing must be God. It was this observation that made William of Ockham, less than a hundred years later, to draw the far reaching conclusion that if every essence or quiddity can be understood without anything being known of its existing, then no amount of knowledge could possibly tell us whether it actually existed. The conclusion drawn from this was that one would never be able to know that anything actually exists. From the ensuing doubt that Ockham raised about the existence of objects, it follows that the existence of God is likewise cast in doubt. Our knowledge of things is based upon the existence of objects. Even if the external existence of objects remain problematic, at least their being in thought is known. But their being in thought, which constitute 'formal' knowledge, can also possibly be caused, as such, by an efficient cause other than the actually existing objects — such as by God, or by the very nature of the mind itself — and hence, the problem as to the 'objective' reality of ideas become more complicated for philosophy and cannot be established by it. Ultimately this trend of philosophy naturally led to consequences resulting in the casting of doubt also on knowledge of the essence of the creatures, and not merely its existence. The epistemological consequences of doubting the existence and essence of objects created the 'problem of God'. After Ockham, Descartes, following the logical course of deduction from the observation of Aquinas, sought to establish the existence of the self by his famous *cogito* argument, from which he ultimately based his *a priori* certainty for the existence of God. But his failure to *prove* the existence of God led to the

---

15 See T. Izutsu's profound analysis of this problem in his *The Concept and Reality of Existence*, Tokyo, 1971; also P.Morewedge, *The Metaphysics of Avicenna*, New York, 1973. See also W.E. Carlo, *The Ultimate Reducibility of Essence to Existence in Existential Metaphysics*, the Hague, 1966.

problem becoming more acute. Descartes established the existence of the self, the existence of the individual creature, man, to himself by means of empirical intuition; this does not necessarily establish the existence of objects outside of thought. In the case of the existence of God, the more impossibly complicated it became, seeing that unlike man He is not subject to empirical intuition. Now what is more problematic about the existence of God is that since His being in thought, His Essence, cannot be known, and since His Being is identical with His Existence, it follows that His Existence also cannot be known. His Existence — in the correspondence theory of truth — can be known only if the identity of His Being and His Existence can be demonstrated rationally, which is not possible to accomplish. At least up till the present time the idea that God's Existence can *rationally* be demonstrated is only a matter of *faith.* Philosophically, and according to the development of thought flowing from Christian Aristotelianism, which some would prefer to refer to more properly as Aristotelian Christianity, the unknowability of God, of His Existence, and of other metaphysical notions about reality and truth was finally established in the West in the 18th century by the German philosopher Immanuel Kant.[16]

To augment this problem of self-evolved doubt about God, the God they have conceived since the earliest periods in the development of Christian dogma was formulated on the basis of a highly improbable conceptual amalgam consisting of the *theos* of Greek philosophy, the *yahweh* of the Hebrews, the *deus* of Western metaphysics, and a host of other traditional *gods* of the pre-Christian Germanic

---

16 On the formation and development of the problems and conceptions mentioned in the above paragraph, see W. Windelband's *A History of Philosophy,* translated by J.H. Tufts, New York, 1953, parts I to VI. As an introductory reading to the relevant periods, see W.H. Wright's *A History of Modern Philosophy,* New York, 1954, chapters I to XII.

traditions. What is now happening is that these separate and indeed mutually conflicting concepts, artificially fused together into an ambiguous whole, are each coming apart, thus creating the heightening crisis in their belief in a God which has already been confused from the very beginning. Furthermore they understand Christianity as historical, and since the doctrine of the Trinity is an integral part of it, their difficulty is further augmented by the necessity that whatever be the formulation of any new Christian theism that might possibly emerge, it must be cast in the Trinitarian crucible. The notion of *person* in the Augustinian concept of the Trinity is left vague, and although Boethius and Aquinas and others through the centuries till the present time have attempted to define it, the problem, like the Gordian Knot, has naturally become more complicated and elusive. In spite of their concession that very real limitations inhere in Hellenism and that modern Western culture has transcended Scholasticism, they argue that, rather than succumb to the philosophical reduction of God to a mere concept, or to a vague and nebulous presence, the vagueness of their early predecessors must be interpreted as indicating the direction in which 'development' is to be pursued. In this way the Hellenic thought structure is conveniently made to appear as 'open ended' and not 'closed' or impeding 'development', so that it might readily be adapted to the equally 'open ended' Christian theism that may be envisaged from time to time as human 'evolution' in line with historical 'development' demands. Thus as long as God is conceived of as Three of Something it would always allow for future change with the changing world in a relativistic fashion; and this relativism allows the believer to be free to conceive whatever notion of God fancies him most, that is the scriptural, or the patristic (hellenic), or the mediaeval (scholastic), or the modern (existential?) in such wise that it also allows him or her to align with 'contemporary experience', which is historically minded. Aside from this and because of the problematic nature of their concept of God, the very name

'God' itself is now becoming problematic for them, to such an extant that they even contemplate discarding it altogether and leaving it to history to coin a new name for connoting a more relevant and adequate concept to refer to the ultimate presence and reality in which they believe.

II

SECULAR-SECULARIZATION-SECULARISM

In the preceding pages I have tried to convey in brief outline and cursory sketch the real contemporary situation in the Western Christian world. Although the sketch is very brief I believe that it has at least captured in summary and true perspective the essential components comprising the fundamental problems that beset Western Christian society. We must see, in view of the fact that secularization is not merely confined to the Western world, that their experience of it and their attitude towards it is most instructive for Muslims. Islām is not similar to Christianity in this respect that secularization, in the way in which it is also happening in the Muslim world, has not and will not necessarily affect our beliefs in the same way it does the beliefs of Western man. For that matter Islām is not the same as Christianity, whether as a religion or as a civilization. But problems arising out of secularization, though not the same as those confronting the West, have certainly caused much confusion in our midst. It is most significant to us that these problems are caused due to the introduction of Western ways of thinking and judging and believing emulated by some Muslim scholars and intellectuals who have been unduly influenced by the West and overawed by its scientific and technological achievements, who by virtue of the fact that they can be thus influenced betray their lack of true understanding and full grasp of both the Islamic as well as the Western world views and essential

15

beliefs and modes of thought that project them; who have, because of their influential positions in Muslim society, become conscious or unconscious disseminators of unnecessary confusion and ignorance. The situation in our midst can indeed be seen as critical when we consider the fact that the Muslim Community is generally unaware of what the secularizing process implies. It is therefore essential that we obtain a clear understanding of it from those who know and are conscious of it, who believe and welcome it, who teach and advocate it to the world.

The term *secular*, from the Latin *saeculum*, conveys a meaning with a marked dual connotation of *time* and *location*; the time referring to the 'now' or 'present' sense of it, and the location to the 'world' or 'worldly' sense of it. Thus *saeculum* means 'this age' or 'the present time', and this age or the present time refers to events in this world, and it also then means 'contemporary events'. The emphasis of meaning is set on a particular time or period in the world viewed as a *historical process.* The concept *secular* refers to the *condition* of the world at this particular time or period or age. Already here we discern the germ of meaning that easily develops itself naturally and logically into the existential context of an ever-changing world in which there occurs the notion of relativity of human values. This spatio-temporal connotation conveyed in the concept secular is derived historically out of the experience and consciousness born of the fusion of the Graeco-Roman and Judaic traditions in Western Christianity. It is this 'fusion' of the mutually conflicting elements of the Hellenic and Hebrew world views which have deliberately been incorporated into Christianity that modern Christian theologians and intellectuals recognize as problematic, in that the former views existence as basically *spatial* and the latter as basically *temporal* in such wise that the arising confusion of worldviews becomes the root of their epistemological and hence also theological problems. Since the world has only in modern times been more and more understood and recognized by them as historical, the emphasis on the temporal aspect of it has become more meaningful and has conveyed a special significance to them. For this reason they exert themselves in efforts emphasizing their conception of the Hebrew vision of existence, which they think is more congenial with the spirit of 'the times', and denouncing the Hellenic as a grave and basic mistake, as can be glimpsed from the brief sketch in the preceding chapter.

Secularization is defined as the deliverance of man "first from religious and then from metaphysical control over his reason and his language".[17] It is "the loosing of the world from religious and quasi-religious understandings of itself, the dispelling of all closed world views, the breaking of all supernatural myths and sacred symbols... the 'defatalization of history', the discovery by man that he has been left with the world on his hands, that he can no longer blame fortune or the furies for what he does with it....; [it is] man turning his attention away from the worlds beyond and toward this world and this time".[18] Secularization encompasses not only the political and social aspects of life, but also inevitably the cultural, for it denotes "the disappearance of religious determination of the symbols of cultural integration".[19] It implies "a historical process, almost certainly irreversible, in which society and culture are delivered from tutelage to religious control and closed metaphysical world views".[20] It is a "liberating development", and the end product of secularization is historical relativism.[21] Hence according to them history is a process of

---

17 By the Dutch theologian Cornelis van Peursen, who occupied the chair of philosophy in the University of Leiden. This definition is cited by the Harvard theologian Harvey Cox in his *The Secular City*, New York, 1965, p. 2, and is quoted from a report on a conference held at the Ecumenical Institute of Bossey, Switzerland, in September, 1959 (see *ibid.*, p. 13, note I).

18 Cox, *ibid*, pp. 2 and 17.

19 *Ibid.*, p. 20

20 *Loc. cit.*

21 *Ibid.*, pp. 30–36.

secularization.[22] The integral components in the dimensions of secularization are the disenchantment of nature, the desacralization of politics, and the deconsecration of values.[23] By the 'disenchantment' of nature — a term and concept borrowed from the German sociologist Max Weber[24] — they mean as he means, the freeing of nature from its religious overtones; and this involves the dispelling of animistic spirits and gods and magic from the natural world, separating it from God and distinguishing man from it, so that man may no longer regard nature as a divine entity, which thus allows him to act freely upon nature, to make use of it according to his needs and plans, and hence create historical change and 'development'. By the 'desacralization' of politics they mean the abolition of sacral legitimation of political power and authority, which is the prerequisite of political change and hence also social change allowing for the emergence of the historical process. By the 'deconsecration' of values they mean the rendering transient and relative all cultural creations and every value system which for them includes religion and worldviews having ultimate and final significance, so that in this way history, the future, is open to change, and man is free to create the change and immerse himself in the 'evolutionary' process. This attitude towards values demands an awareness on the part of secular man of the relativity of his own views and beliefs; he must live with the realization that the rules and ethical codes of conduct

---

22 *Ibid., passim,* and see p. 109.

23 *Ibid.,* pp. 21–23.

24 The phrase 'disenchantment of the world' was used by Freidrich Schiller and quoted by Weber. Another term which Weber used in this connection is rationalization. See Weber's *Essays in Sociology,* New York 1958, see also his *Sociology of Religion,* Boston, 1964. See chapter III and V of the former; and for Weber's concept of rationalization, see Talcott Parson's explanation of it in the Introduction to the latter work, pp. xxxi–xxxiii.

which guide his own life will change with the times and generations. This attitude demands what they call 'maturity', and hence secularization is also a process of 'evolution' of the consciousness of man from the 'infantile' to the 'mature' states, and is defined as "the removal of juvenile dependence from every level of society.... the process of maturing and assuming responsibility.... the removal of religious and metaphysical supports and putting man on his own".[25] They say that this change of values is also the recurrent phenomenon of "conversion" which occurs "at the intersection of the action of history on man and the action of man on history", which they call "responsibility, the acceptance of adult accountability".[26] Now we must take due notice of the fact that they make a distinction between secularization and *secularism*, saying that whereas the former implies a continuing and open-ended process in which values and worldviews are continually revised in accordance with 'evolutionary' change in history, the latter, like religion, projects a closed worldview and an absolute set of values in line with an ultimate historical purpose having a final significance for man. Secularism according to them denotes an *ideology*.[27] Whereas the ideology that is secularism, like the process that is secularization, also disenchants nature and desacralizes politics, it never quite deconsecrates values since it sets up its own system of values intending it to be regarded as absolute and final, unlike secularization which relativises *all* values and produces the openness and freedom necessary for human action and for history. For this reason they regard secularism as a menace to secularization, and urge that it must be vigilantly watched and checked and prevented from becoming the ideology of the state. Secularization, they think, describes the inner workings of man's 'evolution'. The context in which secularization occurs is the urban civilization. The

---

25 Cox, *ibid.*, pp. 109; 119.
26 *Ibid.*, p. 123.
27 *Ibid.*, p. 21.

structure of common life, they believe, has 'evolved' from the primitive to the tribal to the village to the town to the city by stages — from the simple social groupings to the complex mass society; and in the state of human life, or the stage of man's 'evolution', this corresponds to the 'development' of man from the 'infantile' to the 'mature' states. The urban civilization is the context in which the state of man's 'maturing' is taking place; the context in which secularization takes place, patterning the form of the civilization as well as being patterned by it.

The definition of secularization which describes its true nature to our understanding corresponds exactly with what is going on in the spiritual and intellectual and rational and physical and material life of Western man and his culture and civilization; and it is true only when applied to describe the nature and existential condition of Western culture and civilization. The claim that secularization has its roots in biblical faith and that it is the fruit of the Gospel has no substance in historical fact. Secularization has its roots not in biblical faith, but in the *interpretation* of biblical faith by Western man; it is not the fruit of the Gospel, but is the fruit of the long history of philosophical and metaphysical conflict in the religious and purely rationalistic *worldview* of Western man. The interdependence of the interpretation and the worldview operates in history and is seen as a 'development'; indeed it has been so logically in history because for Western man the truth, or God Himself, has become incarnate in man in time and in history.

Of all the great religions of the world Christianity alone shifted its center of origin from Jerusalem to Rome, symbolizing the beginnings of the *westernization* of Christianity and its gradual and successive permeation of Western elements that in subsequent periods of its history produced and accelerated the momentum of secularization. There were, and still are from the Muslim point of view, two Christianities: the original and true one, and the Western version of it. Original and true Christianity conformed with Islām. Those who before the advent of Islām believed in the

original and true teachings of Jesus (on whom be Peace!)
were true believers *(mu'min* and *muslim)*. After the advent
of Islām they would, if they had known the fact of Islām and
if their belief *(īmān)* and submission *(islām)* were truly
sincere, have joined the ranks of Islām. Those who from the
very beginning had altered the original and departed from
the true teaching of Jesus (Peace be upon him!) were the
creative initiators of Western Christianity, the Christianity
now known to us. Since their holy scripture, the Gospel, is
derived partly from the original and true revelation of Jesus
(upon whom be Peace!), the Holy Qur'ān categorizes them
as belonging to the People of the Book *(Ahl al-Kitāb)*.
Among the People of the Book, and with reference to
Western Christianity, those who inwardly did not profess
real belief in the doctrines of the Trinity, the Incarnation
and the Redemption and other details of dogma connected
with these doctrines, who privately professed belief in God
alone and in the Prophet Jesus (on whom be Peace!), who
set up regular prayer to God and did good works in the way
they were spiritually led to do, who while in this condition
of faith were truly and sincerely *unaware* of Islām, were
those referred to in the Holy Qur'ān as nearest in love to
the Believers in Islām.[28] To this day Christians like these and
other People of the Book like them are found among
mankind; and it is to such as these that the term *mu'min*
(believer) is also sometimes applied in the Holy Qur'ān.

Because of the confusion caused by the permeation of
Western elements, the religion from the outset and as it
developed resolutely resisted and diluted the original and
true teachings of Christianity. Neither the Hebrews nor the
original Christians understood or knew or were even
conscious of the presently claimed so called 'radicalism' of
the religion as understood in the modern sense after its
development and secularization as Western Christianity,
and the modern interpretation based upon reading — or

---

28 *Al-Mā'idah* (5): 85–88.

rather misreading — contemporary experience and consciousness into the spirit and thought of the past is nothing but conjecture. The evidence of history shows early Christianity as consistently opposed to secularization, and this opposition, engendered by the demeaning of nature and the divesting of it of its spiritual and theological significance, continued throughout its history of the losing battle against the secularizing forces entrenched paradoxically within the very threshold of Western Christianity. The separation of Church and State, of religious and temporal powers was never the result of an attempt on the part of Christianity to bring about secularization; on the contrary, it was the result of the secular Western philosophical attitude set against what it considered as the anti-secular encroachment of the ambivalent Church based on the teachings of the eclectic religion. The separation represented for Christianity a *status quo* in the losing battle against secular forces; and even that *status quo* was gradually eroded away so that today very little ground is left for the religion to play any significant social and political role in the secular states of the Western world. Moreover the Church when it wielded power was always vigilant in acting against scientific enquiry and purely rational investigation of truth, which seen in the light of present circumstances brought about by such 'scientific' enquiry and 'rational' investigation as it developed in Western history is, however, partly now seen to be justifiable. Contrary to secularization Christianity has always preached a 'closed' metaphysical world view, and it did not really 'deconsecrate' values including idols and icons; it assimilated them into its own mould. Furthermore it involved itself consciously in sacral legitimation of political power and authority, which is anathema to the secularizing process. The westernization of Christianity, then, marked the beginning of its secularization. Secularization is the result of the misapplication of Greek philosophy in Western theology and metaphysics, which in the 17th century logically led to the scientific revolution enunciated by Descartes, who opened the doors to doubt and skepticism; and successively in the 18th and 19th centuries and in our own times, to atheism and agnosticism; to utilitarianism, dialectical materialism, evolutionism and historicism. Christianity has attempted to resist secularization but has failed, and the danger is that having failed to contain it the influential modernist theologians are now urging Christians to join it. Their fanciful claim that the historical process that made the world secular has its roots in biblical faith and is the fruit of the Gospel must be seen as an ingenious way of attempting to extricate Western Christianity from its own self-originated dilemmas. While it is no doubt ingenious it is also self-destructive, for this claim necessitates the accusation that for the past two millenia Christians including their apostles, saints, theologians, theorists and scholars had misunderstood and misinterpreted the Gospel, had made a grave fundamental mistake thereby, and had misled Christians in the course of their spiritual and intellectual history. And this is in fact what they who make the claim say. If what they say is accepted as valid, how then can they and Christians in general be *certain* that those early Christians and their followers throughout the centuries who misunderstood, misinterpreted, mistook and misled on such an important, crucial matter as the purportedly secular message of the Gospel and secularizing mission of the Church, *did not also* misunderstand, misinterpret, mistake and mislead on the paramount, vital matter of the religion and belief itself; on the doctrine of the Trinity; on the doctrine of the Incarnation; on the doctrine of the Redemption and on the *reporting* and *formulation* and *conceptualization* of the revelation? Since it ought to be a matter of absolute, vital importance for them to believe that the report of the very early Christians about the nature of the God Who revealed Himself to them was true, it would be futile for them to overcome this problem by resorting to belief in human 'evolution' and historicity and the relativity of truths according to the experience and consciousness of each stage of human 'evolution' and history, for we cannot accept an answer based merely on subjective experience and consciousness and 'scientific' conjecture where no criteria for knowledge and certainty exist. What they say amounts to meaning that God sent His revelation or revealed Himself to man when man was in his 'infantile' stage of 'evolution'. 'Infantile' man then interpreted the revelation and conceptualized it in dogmatic and doctrinal forms expressing his faith in them. Then when man 'matures' he finds the dogmatic and doctrinal conceptualizations of 'infantile' man no longer adequate for him to express his faith in his time, and so he must develop them as he develops, otherwise they become inadequate. Thus they maintain that the dogmatic and doctrinal conceptualizations 'evolve', but they 'evolve' not because they are from the very beginning necessarily inadequate, but because as man 'develops' they become inadequate if they fail to develop correspondingly. This in our view of course does not solve the problem of the reliability of the *reporting* of the revelation, the more so when it was the work of 'infantile' man. Moreover this way of integrating religion with the evolutionary theory of development seems to lead logically to circular reasoning. Why should God send His revelation or reveal Himself to 'infantile' man and not to 'mature' man, especially since God, Who created man, must know the stage of growth at which he was at the moment of the revelation? Even a man would not send a vitally important message or reveal himself meaningfully to an infant. They may answer that God did not send His revelation or reveal Himself to 'mature' man but to 'infantile' man instead precisely in order to initiate the process of 'maturing' in him so that when he 'developed' to 'maturity' he would be able to know its true meaning and purpose. But then, even in his allegedly 'mature' stage in this modern, secular age, Western man is still inadequately informed about God, and still groping for a meaning in God. It seems then that Western man who believes in this version of Christianity must either admit that man is *still* 'infantile', or that the revelation or the conceptualization of its meaning and purpose is from the very beginning necessarily inadequate. As regards the revelation itself, it would be impossible for them to ascertain beyond doubt that it was reliably formulated and reported, for there exists other reports, apart from that of St. Barnabas, and both from the Ante-Nicene and Post-Nicene Fathers, which contradicted the report on which the conceptualization which became the 'official' version of Christianity now known to us is based.

Western man is always inclined to regard his culture and civilization as man's cultural vanguard; and his own experience and consciousness as those representative of the most 'evolved' of the species, so that we are all in the process of lagging behind them, as it were, and will come to realize the same experience and consciousness in due course sometime. It is with this attitude that they, believing in their own absurd theories of human evolution, view human history and development and religion and religious experience and consciousness. We reject the validity of the truth of their assertion, with regard to secularization and their experience and consciousness and belief, to speak on our behalf. The secularization that describes its true nature clearly when applied to describe Western man and his culture and civilization cannot be accepted as true if it is intended to be a description of what is happening in and to the world and man in which it is also meant to be applicable to the religion of Islām and the Muslims, and even perhaps to the other Eastern religions and their respective adherents. Islām totally rejects any application to itself of the concepts secular, or secularization, or secularism as they do not belong and are alien to it in every respect; and they belong and are natural only to the intellectual history of Western-Christian religious experience and consciousness. We do not, unlike Western Christianity, lean heavily for theological and metaphysical support on the theories of secular philosophers, metaphysicians, scientists, paleontologists, anthropologists, sociologists, psychoanalysts, mathematicians, linguists and other such scholars, most of whom, if not all, did not even practise the religious life, who knew not nor believed in religion without doubt and vacillation; who were skeptics, agnostics, atheists, and doubters all. In the case of religion we say that in order to know it man's self itself becomes the 'empirical' subject of his own 'empiricism', so that his study and scrutiny of himself is as a science based upon research, investigation and observation of the self by itself in the course of its faith and sincere subjugation to Revealed Law. Knowledge about religion and religious experience is therefore not merely obtained by purely rational specu-lation and reflection alone. Metaphysics as we understand it is a science of Being involving not only contemplation and intellectual reflection, but is based on knowledge gained through practical devotion to that Being Whom we contemplate and sincerely serve in true submission according to a clearly defined system of Revealed Law. Our objection that their authorities, on whose thoughts are based the formulation and interpretation of the facts of human life and existence, are not reliable and acceptable insofar as religion is concerned on the ground stated above is valid enough already. We single out religion because we cannot discuss the issue of secularization without first coming to grips, as it were, with religion by virtue of the fact that religion is the fundamental element in human life and existence against which secularization is working. Now in their case it seems that they have found it difficult to define religion, except in terms of historicity and faith vaguely expressed, and have accepted instead the definition of their secular authorities who when they speak of religion refer to it as part of culture, of tradition; as a system of beliefs and practices and attitudes and values and aspi-rations that are created out of history and the confron-tation of man and nature, and that 'evolve' in history and undergo a process of 'development', just as man himself 'evolves' and undergoes a process of 'development'. In this way secularization as they have defined it will of course be viewed by the theists among them as a critical problem for religion precisely because man believes that his belief cast in a particular form — which according to the atheists is an illusion — is real and permanent; whereas in point of fact — at least according to the modern theists — it must change and 'develop' as man and history 'develop'. Now the view that religion undergoes 'development' in line with human 'evolution' and historicity is indeed true in their case, just as secularization is true and seen as a historical development in their experience and consciousness.[29] We say this because, from the point of view of Islām, although Western Christianity is *based on revelation*, it is not a *revealed religion* in the sense that Islām is. According to Islām the paramount, vital doctrine of Western Christianity such as the Trinity, the Incarnation and the Redemption and other details of dogma connected with them are all cultural creations which are categorically denied by the Holy Qur'ān as divinely inspired. Not only the Holy Qur'ān, but sources arising within early Christianity itself, as we have just pointed out, denied their divinely inspired origin in such wise that these denials, historically valid as succinct evidence, present weighty grounds for doubting the reliability and authenticity of the reporting and subsequent interpretation and conceptualization of the revelation. The Holy Qur'ān indeed confirms that God sent Jesus (Peace be upon him!) a revelation in the form known as *al-Injīl* (the Evangel), but at the same time denies the authenticity of the revelation as transmitted by the followers of some of the disciples. In the Holy Qur'ān Jesus (on whom be Peace!) was sent as a messenger to the Children of Israel charged with the mission of correcting their deviation from their covenant with God and of confirming that covenant with a

---

29 Even philosophy in the West has now more and more come to be regarded as unable to give a conclusive answer to its permanent question about truth. Philosophy attempts to clarify only the "truth-perspective" of the age in which the crisis of truth occurs, and is hence now regarded as an 'open science'. Advocates of this view are clearly representatives of

second covenant; of conveying Glad Tidings (Gospel) of the approaching advent of the Universal Religion (Islām) which would be established by the Great Teacher whose name he gave as Aḥmad (Muḥammad). The second covenant was meant to be valid until the advent of Islām when the Final and Complete Revelation would abrogate previous revelations and be established among mankind.[30] So in the Holy Qur'ān God did not charge Jesus (on whom be Peace!) with the mission of establishing a *new religion* called Christianity. It was some other disciples and the apostles including chiefly Paul who departed from the original revelation and true teachings based on it, and who began preaching a new religion and set about establishing the foundations for a new religion which later came to be called Christianity. At the beginning even the name 'Christian' was not known to it, and it developed itself historically until its particular traits and characteristics and attributes took form and became fixed and clarified and refined and recognizable as the religion of a culture and civilization known to the world as Christianity. The fact that Christianity also had no Revealed Law (*sharī'ah*) expressed in the teachings, sayings and model actions (i.e., *sunnah*) of Jesus (on whom be Peace!) is itself a most significant indication that Christianity began as a new religion not intended as such by its presumed founder, nor authorized as such by the God Who sent him. Hence Christianity, by virtue of its being created by man, gradually developed its system of rituals by assimilation from other cultures and traditions as well as originating its own fabrications; and

---

the spirit of secularization, which demands 'openness' in every vision of truth. See, for example, G.A. Rauche, *Contemporary Philosophical Alternatives and the Crisis of Truth*, the Hague, 1970.

30 See *al-Mā'idah* (5): 49; 75; 78; 119–121; *Āl 'Imrān* (3): 49–51; 77–79; *al-Nisā'* (4): 157; 171; *al-Tawbah* (9): 30–31; *al-Ra'd* (13): 38–39; *al-Ṣaff* (61): 6; 9; *al-Baqarah* (2): 106; 135–140; *Sabā* (34): 28.

through successive stages clarified its creeds such as those at Nicea, Constantinople and Chalcedon. Since it had no Revealed Law it had to assimilate Roman laws; and since it had no coherent world view projected by revelation, it had to borrow from Graeco-Roman thought and later to construct out of it an elaborate theology and metaphysics. Gradually it created its own specifically Christian cosmology, and its arts and sciences developed within the vision of a distinctly Christian universe and world view.

From its earliest history Western Christianity, as we have pointed out, came under the sway of Roman influences with the concomitant latinization of its intellectual and theological symbols and concepts which were infused with Aristotelian philosophy and worldview and other Western elements that gradually 'disenchanted' nature and deprived it of spiritual significance. This divesting and demeaning of nature to a mere 'thing' of no sacred meaning was indeed the fundamental element that started the process of secularization in Western Christianity and the Western world. Christianity failed to contain and Christianize these elements, and unwittingly, then helplessly, allowed the secularizing developments engendered by alien forces within its very bosom to proceed relentlessly and inexorably along logical lines in philosophy, theology, metaphysics and science until its full critical impact was realized almost too late in modern times.

The Western concept of religion does not in our view come under the category of *revealed* religion in the strict sense as applicable to Islām. We cannot accept, to mention a scientific example, Nathan Söderblom's categorization of Christianity as a revealed religion according to his typology of religion[31]. For us it is for the most part a sophisticated form of culture religion, distinguished only by the fact that it claims possession of a revealed Book which, though partly true, it nevertheless was not intended nor authorized by

---

31 See his *The Nature of Revelation*, London, 1933.

that Book to call upon mankind universally in the manner that a revealed religion was called upon to do from the very beginning without need of further 'development' in the religion itself and its sacred laws. A revealed religion as we understand it is complete and perfect in its adequacy for *mankind* from the very beginning. The Holy Qur'ān says that Islām is already made complete and perfect for mankind, and this claim to completion and perfection is substantiated from its very beginning by history. The name *Islām* was given to the religion from the very beginning just as the name *Muslim* was given to denote the adherents of the religion from the very start. The Revelation itself was completed during the lifetime of the Holy Prophet, who may God bless and give Peace!, who himself interpreted it in his life and whose Sacred Law he patterned in his teachings, his thoughts and sayings and model actions (*sunnah*). Even his Companions and contemporaries acted and behaved in a manner divinely inspired to become the standard and criterion for the future; and they questioned him urgently whilst he was yet among them on every conceivable and actual problem of daily life and right conduct and thought and action and guidance that summarized the needs of mankind and whose answers would suffice for man for all ages and generations to come. They all acted in a concerted and significantly knowing manner emphasizing their consciousness that this was the Final Revelation from God, the Ultimate Religion for mankind, the Last Prophet to appear among men. That age in history became the Criterion for the future, as the future truth and values that guide to it were all there, so that Islām and the time of the Holy Prophet (may God bless and give him Peace!) is always relevant, is always adequate, is always 'modern' or new, is always ahead of time because it transcends history. In this way the essentials of what made religion a truly revealed one was completed and perfected, and for this reason we say that Islām knew and recognized its realization from the moment of its actual existence. As such it transcends history and is not subject to the kind of self-searching 'evolution' and 'development' that Christianity experienced and will continue to experience. Though some of us use the terms 'tradition' and 'traditional' in the context of Islām yet these terms do not and are not meant to refer to the kind of tradition that originated in man's creative activity which evolves in history and consists of culture[32]. They always refer to the Holy Prophet, who may God bless and give Peace!, and to the religious way and method of the Prophets of the Abrahamic 'tradition'; and this tradition is originated by revelation and instruction from God, not created and passed on by man in history. So now we who follow that religious way and method are following that 'tradition'. Since Islām is the religion which transcends the influences of human 'evolution' and historicity, the values embodied in it are absolute; and this means that Islām has its own absolute vision of God, of the Universe, of Reality, of Man; its own ontological, cosmological, psychological interpretation of reality; its own world view and vision of the Hereafter having a final significance for mankind. As such therefore it completely rejects the notion of 'deconsecration' of values if that were to mean the relativization of *all* values continually recurring in history as they mean. Islām certainly deconsecrates all values in the sense of all *unislamic* values; in the sense of values that run counter to Islām and to the truth which is partially found in the other world religions and in the good traditions of man and his society (*al ma'rūf*). There cannot be for Islām a deconsecration of every value system including its own, because in Islām all value systems that need deconsecration, all human and cultural creations including idols and icons, have *already* been deconsecrated by it so that there is need of no further 'evolution' of values, or of relativization of values, since its values which include the truth as partially found in other world religions and in the good in man and his society, are already the ultimate for mankind. The same is the case with the 'desacralization' of

---

32 We are referring here to the concept of *naql.*

politics, of political power and authority. In Islām, more so even than in Christianity, the desacralization of politics was not originally just an idea that came to be gradually realized in history; it was recognized from the very beginning and began with Islām itself. Islām indeed desacralizes politics, but not to the extent they mean, for Islām itself is based on Divine Authority and on the sacred authority of the Holy Prophet (may God bless and give him Peace!), which is no less than the reflection of God's Authority, and on the authority of those who emulate his example. Thus every Muslim individually, and collectively as society and nation and as a Community (*ummah*) all deny to anyone, to any government and state, sacral legitimacy unless the person or the government or the state conforms with the practice of the Holy Prophet (may God bless and give him Peace!) and follow the injunctions of the Sacred Law revealed by God. Indeed, the Muslim in fact does not owe real allegiance and loyalty even to legitimate king and country and state; his real allegiance and fealty and loyalty is to God and to His Prophet to the exclusion of all else. And the same is true with regard to the 'disenchantment' of nature, which is the most fundamental component in the dimensions of secularization. It is the disenchantment of nature that brought about the chaos of secularization which is ravaging the Western world and Christianity in contemporary life; and because the crisis caused is so ominously portentious for the future of man and his world — seeing that secularization is becoming a global crisis — I think it proper to show in brief and generalized but fairly accurate sketch the salient features marking its origins and history of development in the Western world.[33]

---

33 The following sketch outlined from page 33 to 38 is most cursory. For a fuller treatment of this subject, see S.II. Nasr's Man and Nature, London, 1976.

Before the rise of Christianity, in the Olympian age of Antiquity nature was not separated from the gods. But when degeneration and decadence of religion began to set in among the Greeks, the gods were gradually banished from nature, which then became devoid of spiritual significance. Originally the Greek cosmology, like those of the other peoples of Antiquity, was permeated with spiritual forces governing and maintaining and sustaining the universe. Their philosophers sought to discover the underlying principle — what they called the *archē* — the spiritual substance that forms the ground of all reality. As the gods were driven away from their respective domains in nature, Greek philosophy was transformed from the symbolic interpretation of nature to become more and more concerned with explaining nature in plain naturalistic and purely rational terms reducing its origin and reality to mere natural causes and forces. When Aristotle introduced Greek philosophy to the Roman world where Christianity was later to formulate and establish itself as the religion of the Roman Empire and of the West, this pure rationalism and concomitant naturalism, stripping nature of its spiritual meaning that the intellect alone could recognize and seek to fathom, were already prevalent factors in the interpretation of the Roman worldview. No doubt other forms of philosophy that recognized the spiritual significance of nature, a contemplative intellectualism or metaphysics, still existed in both the Greek and Roman worlds, but Aristotelianism held sway over the rest, so that by the time Christianity appeared on the scene pure rationalism and naturalism had already dominated the life and mind of the Latin peoples. Christianity itself came under the influence of this naturalistic portrayal of nature devoid of symbolic significance, and reacted to this influence by demeaning the Kingdom of Nature and neglecting serious contemplation of it in favour of the Kingdom of God having no connection whatever with the world of nature. That is why the only connection that could happen between the two Kingdoms in Christianity would *logically* be the supernatural one. Elements of Greek cosmology which stressed the paramount role of the intelligence as the prime means by which man is able to interpret the spiritual significance of nature were then still prevalent, and this obviously led to a confrontation with Christian theology which had come under the sway of naturalistic rationalism. The outcome of this religio-philosophical confrontation was that Christian theology began to suppress the role of intelligence, and hence also the knowledge of spiritual truth, and at the same time urged unquestioning faith through the exercise not of human intelligence and reason but of sheer human will which made love the basis of faith. Thus knowledge and certainty, which are both aspects of the same truth and which constitute the very essence of the intellect, was relegated to a somewhat inferior status in comparison with a purely rational theology. We have distinguished the intelligence or the intellect from the rational mind or reason in this way in order to describe the case in Western intellectual history. In our view, however, the intelligence is both the intellect (*al-'aql*) as well as its projection in the human mind which creates and organizes its mental activity, that is, the ratio or reason which we also designate as *'aql*. The fact that we use the same term to designate both concepts demonstrates that we make neither dichotomy nor separation between the activities of the two aspects of the same cognitive principle in man. Thus it is therefore obvious that when we apply in English the same term 'rational' to describe an aspect of Islām, we do not mean the same thing as when the same term is applied in the discussion of Western intellectual history and its influence on Christian theology and metaphysics and on the development of Christianity as in the above case. What is considered 'rational' in Islām does not merely pertain to the mind's systematic and logical interpretation of the facts of experience; or its rendering intelligible and manageable to reason the data of experience; or its abstraction of facts and data and their relationships; or the grasping of nature by the mind, and the law-giving operation the mind renders upon nature. Since reason is a projection of the intellect, it functions in conformity with the intellect, which is a spiritual substance inherent in the spiritual organ of cognition known as the 'heart' (*al-qalb*). Hence the understanding of spiritual realities is also within the province of reason and is not necessarily divorced from rational understanding of them. In the case of Christian theology and its latinized vocabulary the two terms *intellectus* and *ratio* corresponding with sapiential and scientific knowledge respectively, have been understood not as being in conformity with each other, and each has been stressed over the other in different periods of its history; the *intellectus* in the case of Augustine, and the *ratio* in the case of Aquinas. Christian theology suppressed the sapiential role of the intellect and stressed the scientific role of the purely rational, which can only operate on nature devoid of spiritual significance and follow its own naturalistic logic to its final conclusion. Once the rational became more or less severed from the intellectual, the world of nature is seen as a material, physical object with no connection with the spiritual reality and truth underlying it. As such nature became rejected as it was of no use and even obstructive to the Christian endeavour to attain to the world of spirit. It was inevitable that Aristotelianism became absorbed into Christian theology and metaphysics, and this assimilation of Aristotelian philosophy into Christian theology was finally accomplished in the 13th century when Aquinas achieved what came to be known in the intellectual history of the West as the Thomistic Synthesis. Rational philosophy and theology, without the intellectual criterion, naturally led to doubt about the existence of objects as Ockham, deriving from the Thomistic metaphysics of being, was to demonstrate soon after.[34] In the development of science in the West, the logical result of this rationalism and secularization of nature was highlighted by the Copernican revo-

---

34 See above pp. 9–12. See also Dewart, *The Future of Belief*, pp. 152–159.

lution in physics in which the decentralization of the earth in the cosmos brought repercussions that reduced the importance of man himself therein. It finally led to man being deprived of cosmic significance; he became terrestrialized and his transcendence was denied him. Already in the Western Christian world view he was conceived as a fallen creature, and this terrestrialization indeed seemed to conform with the salvific purport assigned to the doctrine of Redemption. Perhaps more important in its secularizing effect to the development of science in the West, the Cartesian revolution in the 17th century effected a final dualism between matter and spirit in a way which left nature open to the scrutiny and service of secular science, and which set the stage for man being left only with the world on his hands. Western philosophy developed resolutely and logically alongside the secularizing science. Man began to be conceived more and more in terms emphasizing his humanity, individuality and freedom. Already he was rid of the gods of nature who all fled from his rational onslaughts which made nature natural for him to act upon, and now his self-assertion by means of a secularizing philosophy and science sought to wrench his freedom from the God of the Universe so that he might act freely upon the nature confronting him. While in the 17th and 18th centuries Christian philosophers still believed in the possibility of a science of metaphysics with which to interpret and prove the reality of spiritual truths such as God, the soul and its immortality, the world as a whole, the trend and methods of secular thought and logic had already penetrated, as we have briefly seen, into its metaphysical structure at least since the 13th century. In the 15th and 16th centuries, during the period known as the Renaissance, Western man seemed already to have lost interest in Christianity as a religion. They engaged eagerly in the pursuit of knowledge and the revival of ancient civilization which they were beginning to acquaint themselves with again after what was to them a period of decay, a period in which Christianity seemed included.

They emphasized the importance of the newly discovered ancient sources and rejected mediaeval standards and methods. They were thrilled by the 'discovery' of the world and of man, and lost interest in mediaeval theology and metaphysics as the interpreter of reality in favour of the 'new' or modern scientific interpretation. In this interpretation they laid emphasis on man and his place in the universe. The very name *renaissance*, which means 'to be born', surely reflects the intellectual atmosphere of the period in which Western man felt himself being born into a new world of new possibilities; a new realization of his powers and potentials. From the 17th to the 19th centuries the European Enlightenment was related to, and indeed was a continuation of the Renaissance. This period was characterized by its zeal for the materialization and secularization of the ideal man in an ideal society. Naturalist philosophers wrote on natural law, natural religion, and stressed humanity, freedom, liberty, justice. Their ideas were turned to reality in America and served as the basic philosophy of Independence. If *renaissance* means 'to be born', then *enlightenment* refers to Western man's 'coming of age' from the state of infancy in which his reason had to depend on the aid of others, but which is now realized as matured and fully fledged to lead on its own. Thus while Christian philosophers sought to erect a science of metaphysics, they were in fact — by virtue of the secular elements that had since many centuries penetrated into its metaphysical structure — only leading their metaphysics towards final dissolution, corroded, as it were, from within by those very elements it harboured. Christianity was ultimately blamed as having forfeited the confidence of Western man in 'revealed' religion. After Kant in the 18th century, metaphysics was considered an unnecessary and deceptive guide to reality and truth which should be abandoned by rational, thinking men, as it was demonstrated by philosophy that spiritual realities and truths cannot be known and proved, and that none can be certain of their existence. It is the fruits of secularizing philosophy and science, which were altogether alien to the soil of true Christianity, which eventually led Western man to believe in human evolution and historicity. Now in our time that belief and secularization going hand in hand has almost supplanted Western Christianity in the heart and mind of Western man. The disenchantment of nature and terrestrialization of man has resulted, in the former case, in the reduction of nature to a mere object of utility having only a functional significance and value for scientific and technical management and for man; and in the latter case, in the reduction of man of his transcendent nature as spirit emphasizing his humanity and physical being, his secular knowledge and power and freedom, which led to his deification, and so to his reliance upon his own rational efforts of enquiry into his origins and final destiny, and upon his own knowledge thus acquired which he now sets up as the criterion for judging the truth or falsehood of his own assertions.

It is clear then that the disenchantment of nature understood in the sense derived from the historical development of secular philosophy and science and its influence upon Western Christian theology as sketched above is most certainly opposed to the Islamic view of nature. The Holy Qur'ān declares in no uncertain terms that the whole of nature is as it were a great, open Book to be understood and interpreted. The Holy Qur'ān also says that those among mankind who possess intelligence, insight, understanding, discernment, knowledge, know the meaning of that Book, for nature is like a book that tells us about the Creator; it 'speaks' to man as a revelation of God. The Holy Qur'ān's description of nature and man — both in their outward manifestation and their inward hiddenness — as *āyāt* (words, sentences, signs, symbols) is self-explanatory in that respect. Nature has cosmic meaning and must, because of its symbolical connection with God, be respected. Man according to the Holy Qur'ān is God's vicegerent (*khalīfah*) and inheritor of the Kingdom of Nature. This does not mean that he should be presumptuous enough to regard himself as "copartner with God in creation" as some modernist and even traditional Western Christian theologians think. He must treat nature justly; there must be harmony between him and nature. Since he has been entrusted with the stewardship of the Kingdom of Nature which belongs to God, he must look after it and make legitimate use of it, and not ruin and spread chaos over it. If nature is like a great, open Book then we must learn the meaning of the Words in order to discern their tentative and final purposes and enact their biddings and invitations and instructions to beneficial use in such wise that we may come to know and acknowledge in grateful appreciation the overwhelming generosity and wisdom of the incomparable Author. It is not surprising, though regrettable, that Bonaventure of Bagnoregio, a contemporary of Aquinas, never developed this important symbolical significance of nature into Christian theology, for he too did remark that nature is like an open Book which those who know the meaning of the Words are able to understand and interpret. This remarkable observation by him was undoubtedly derived from the Holy Qur'ān, whose Latin translation was available to him. But it is not surprising that he did not develop the idea into Christian theology because Western Christianity was then not inclined to treat nature respectfully as a subject of study in the intellectual sense. Moreover, and with reference to the intellect, Bonaventure was the leading follower of Augustine who stressed the importance of the intellect in man as the organ of contemplation of higher truths. At that time Aquinas was deeply involved in the defense of Aristotle against Augustinianism and Platonism and Neo-Platonism which predominated among the Averroeist and Avicennan schools in the University of Paris. The ultimate victory went to Aquinas, and Augustinianism along with its stress upon the intellect was vanquished. Only in our day has some notice begun to be made of Bonaventure's observation about nature,[35] albeit only in a rather incidental sort of way

---

35 This was during the International Congress of the VII

without assigning to it centrality and importance. The disenchantment of nature in the sense they mean has divested nature of any cosmic significance and severed its symbolical connection with God; it deprived man's respect for nature to the extent that he treats nature which once held him in awe with a ruthless sort of vindictiveness; it has destroyed the harmony between man and nature. The terrestrialization and secularization of man, his materialization and humanization, has caused him to deconsecrate his values; to deify himself and without real authority and wisdom to play the role of creator, and that made him unjust to nature — both human nature which includes spirit and the world of nature. It is true that the Holy Qur'ān also 'disenchanted' nature from the very moment of its revelation, and we can adduce more sacred verses in clear testi mony of this fact without having to resort to hermeneutics than the modernist Western-Christian theologians can from the Gospel; and yet we shall never be forced to find desperate utterance in compromising the meaning of the Revelation with secularization such that will make us see in those sacred verses the roots of secularization, or that secularization is the fruit of the Holy Qur'ān. Islām 'disenchanted' nature, but only in the sense of, and so far as, banishing the animistic and magical superstitions and beliefs and false gods from nature where indeed they do not belong. Islām did not completely deprive nature of spiritual significance, for its sees in Creation, in the heavens and the earth and what lies between; in the sun and the moon and the stars; in the alternation of night and day; in

---

Centenary of St. Bonaventure of Bagnoregio, held in Rome on the 19–26 of September, 1974, which I attended and of which I was a member. As far as I know, there is one book which treats of the subject of Bonaventure's concept of nature as a Book of God, and this book seems to be the only serious and systematic analysis of the subject in recent times. W. Rauch, *Das Buch Gottes Eine Systematische Untersuchung über des Buchbegriffs bei Bonaventura*, Munchen, 1961.

the fecundating winds and life-giving rains and canopic skies; in the surging, spreading seas and the majestic mountains; in the rivers and fields and the multiplicity of varying colours and qualities; in the sustaining grains and fruits and in the animals and plants and minerals; in all these and their outer and inner workings and in the forces of nature and many more that we do not know; in man and his mate of like nature and the love set between them; in our creation and procreation, our ships and habitations and fabrications; in every thing in the farthest horizons and in our very selves — the Signs of God.[36] The phenomenon of Islām and its impact in the history of world cultures and civilizations did in our view bring about the *proper* disenchantment of nature, and the *proper* desacralization of politics, and the *proper* deconsecration of values, and hence without bringing about with it secularization. Not only is secularization as a whole the expression of an utterly unislamic worldview, it is also set against Islām, and Islām totally rejects the explicit as well as implicit manifestation and ultimate significance of secularization; and Muslims must therefore vigorously repulse it wherever it is found among them and in their minds, for it is as deadly poison to true faith (*īmān*). The nearest equivalent to the concept secular is connoted by the Quranic concept of *al-ḥayāt al-dunyā*: 'the life of the world', or 'the worldly life'. The word *dunyā*, derived from *dana*, conveys the meaning of something being 'brought near'; so that the world is that which is *brought near to the sensible and intelligible experience and consciousness of man*. By virtue of the fact that what is brought near — the world — surrounds us, as it were, and overwhelms us, it is bound to distract us from consciousness of our final destination which is beyond it, what comes *after* it: *al-ākhirah* or the Hereafter. Since it comes at the *end*,

---

36 See, for example, *Yūnus* (10): 5–6; *al-Ḥijr* (15): 16; 19–23; 85; *al-Naḥl* (16): 3; 5–8; 10–18; 48; 65–69; 72–74; 78–81; al-*Anbiyā'* (21): 16; *al-Naml* (27): 59–64; *Ghāfir, al-Mu'min* (40): 61; 64; *al-Mulk* (57): 2–5; 15; and *Fuṣṣilat, al-Sajdah* (41): 53.

al-ākhirah is felt as 'far', and this accentuates the distraction created by what is 'near'. The Holy Qur'ān says that the Hereafter is better than the life of the world; it is more abiding, everlasting. But the Holy Qur'ān does not derogate the world itself, or dissuade from contemplation and reflection and interpretation of its wonders; it only warns of the distracting and ephemeral nature of the *life* of the world. The warning emphasis in the concept of 'the life of the world', or 'the worldly life' (*al-ḥayāt al-dunyā*) is the *life* of it, so that the world and nature is not demeaned as in the concept secular. That is why we said that *al-ḥayāt al-dunyā* is the nearest equivalent to 'secular' in the Islamic worldview projected by the Holy Qur'ān. Now since the world is that which is 'brought near', and since the world and nature are Signs of God, it is the Signs of God that are brought near, and it would be blasphemous to derogate the world and nature knowing them in their true purpose. It is the Mercy and Loving Kindness of God that He caused His Signs to be brought near to us, the better for us to understand their meaning. There can be no excuse, therefore, for those who, struck by awe of the Signs, worship them instead of God to whom they point; or those who, seeking God, yet reject the Signs because they see nothing in them but distraction; or again those who, denying God, appropriate the Signs for their own ends and change them in pursuit of illusory 'development'. The world cannot develop as it is already perfect — only life in the world can develop. There is a final end to the world just as there is a final end to life in the world. Development of life in the world is that which leads to success in the Hereafter, for there is no meaning to 'development' unless it is aligned to a final objective.[37] We have said that secularization *as a whole* is not only the expression of an utterly unIslamic world view, but that it is also set against Islām; and yet we have also pointed out that the *integral components* in the dimensions of secularization — that is, the

---

37 See below pp. 86 – 88.

disenchantment of nature, the desacralization of politics, and the deconsecration of values — when seen in their *proper* perspectives, indeed become part of the integral components in the dimensions of Islām, for they reflect one of the fundamental elements in the Islamic vision of reality and existence, and characterize Islām in true and real manifestation in history bringing about the effect that revolutionizes the world view of man. But it must be emphasized that the integral components which to the Western world and Western man and Christianity represent the dimensions of secularization, do not in the same sense represent themselves to Islām in spite of the fact that they exhibit great similarities in their 'style of action' upon man and history. In the same way that a Christian and a Muslim are basically the same insofar as they are human beings and believe in religions which are closely similar to one another, yet it cannot be said, because they are the same in their human characteristics and there are apparent similarities between their religions, that there could be such a thing as Christian Islām or Islamic Christianity, since this would confuse the two religions. Whatever 'Islamic Christianity' or 'Christian Islām' is, it is definitely neither Christianity nor Islām. Christianity is *Christianity* and Islām is *Islām.* So it is manifestly erroneous for Muslims — particularly some '*ulamā*' who follow the so-called 'modernist' trend set by some scholars and intellectuals, and those scholars and intellectuals themselves who have some experience of Western knowledge and culture and civilization, who since the end of the last century and the beginning of this one till our present day have been unduly overawed by Western achievements — to speak, in their well meaning but misguided attempts to elevate the Muslim mind to the level of modern achievements in science and technology and the human sciences and socio-economic realities, of such nonsense as, for example, "Islamic Socialism" or "Socialism in Islām". They confuse Islām and Socialism and are thus responsible for the confusion of Muslims and for leading them astray and causing unnecessary conflict in their midst.

43

Socialism is a separate, secular *ideology*, and there can never be such a reality as 'Islamic Socialism' or 'Socialism in Islām'. If they desire and intend to convey the idea that certain integral components in the dimensions of socialism are parallel with or similar to those in the dimensions of Islām, then they should express the idea in other ways not susceptible of an ambiguous interpretation such as, for example, 'the social, political, and economic dimensions of Islām'— or some other such expressions which could, with a modicum of intellectual effort, be very easily conceived and regarded and accepted as a valid interpretation of the Islamic worldview. But their failure to understand this, and their determination to write as they did, betray clearly their lack of true familiarity with and depth of knowledge of either or both Islām and Western culture and civilization. And as such they constitute a continuing threat to the Muslim Community in its welfare and right guidance. So then in the same way that there can never be an 'Islamic Socialism', so there can never really be an 'Islamic Secularism'; and secularization can never really be a part of Islām. Hence those integral components whose historical and cultural effect in the West pertain to the dimensions of secularization, and which are not necessarily the monopoly of Western culture and civilization because they also play an important historical and cultural role in the impact of Islām in human history and culture, should simply be interpreted in their proper Islamic perspective as the integral components in the dimensions of *islamization*.[38] Islamization is the liberation of man first from magical, mythological, animistic, national-cultural tradition opposed to Islām, and then from secular control over his reason and his language. The man of Islām is he whose reason and language are no longer controlled by magic, mythology, animism, his own national and cultural traditions opposed to Islām, and secularism. He is liberated from both the magical and the

---

38 See below pp. 169 – 183. Appendix, *On Islamization: The Case Of The Malay-Indonesian Archipelago.*

secular world views. We have defined the nature of islamization as a liberating process. It is liberating because since man is both physical being and spirit, the liberation refers to his spirit, for man as such is the real man to whom all conscious and significant actions ultimately refer. The liberation of his spirit or soul bears direct influence upon his physical being or body in that it brings about peace and harmony within himself in his manifestation as a human being, and also between him as such and nature. He has, in liberation in this sense, set his course towards attainment to his original state, which is in harmony with the state of all being and existence (*i.e. fiṭrah*). It is also liberation from subservience to his physical demands which incline toward the secular and injustice to his true self or soul, for man as physical being inclines towards forgetfulness of his true nature, becoming ignorant of his true purpose and unjust to it. Islamization is a process not so much of *evolution* as that of *devolution* to original nature; man as spirit is already perfect, but man as such when actualized as physical being is subject to forgetfulness and ignorance and injustice to himself and hence is not necessarily perfect. His 'evolution' towards perfection is his progress towards realization of his original nature as spirit. Thus in the individual, personal, existential sense islamization refers to what is described above in which the Holy Prophet represents the highest and most perfect Example; in the collective, social and historical sense islamization refers to the Community's striving towards realization of the moral and ethical quality of social perfection achieved during the age of the Holy Prophet (may God bless and give him Peace!) who created it under Divine Guidance. We have also defined islamization as involving first the islamization of language, and this fact is demonstrated by the Holy Qur'ān itself when it was first revealed among the Arabs. Language, thought and reason are closely interconnected and are indeed interdependent in projecting to man his worldview or vision of reality. Thus the islamization of language brings about the islamization of thought and reason, not in the secular sense, but in the sense we have described.[39] The islamization of Arabic by being charged with Divine inspiration in the form of Revelation transformed the place of Arabic among the languages of mankind to become the only divinely inspired living language and is in that sense 'new' and perfected to the superlative degree so that it — especially its basic Islamic vocabulary — is not subject to change and development nor governed by the vicissitudes of social change as in the case of all other languages which derive from culture and tradition. The elevation of Arabic as the language in which God revealed the Holy Qur'ān to mankind caused the language as no other to be preserved unchanged and alive and to remain perpetually as the exalted standard of Arabic, as the linguistic criterion in every respect, exhibiting its highest and most excellent expression. With regard to meaning pertaining to Islām, therefore, every such meaning is governed by the semantic vocabulary of the Holy Qur'ān and not by social change, so that adequate knowledge about Islām is made possible for all at all times and generations, since such knowledge including its ethical, axiological, aesthetical and logical norms is already an established matter, and not one that 'evolves' and 'develops' as man and history allegedly 'evolve' and 'develop'. If there occurs then a sense of inadequacy about Islām and its relevance to changing situations, this illusory sense in reality occurs not because Islām is inadequate or irrelevant, but because the sense of inadequacy and irrelevance arises simply due to forgetfulness (*nisyān*) causing ignorance (*jahl*) which can be remedied by learning and remembrance. Ignorance causes confusion (*ẓulm*), and ignorance and confusion are the results of deislamization, which does occur among Muslims in history. Deislamization is the infusion of alien concepts into the minds of Muslims, where they remain and influence thought and reasoning. It is the causing of forgetfulness of Islām and of the Muslim's duty to God and

---

39 See above, pp. 30 – 32; 38 – 43.

to His Prophet, which is the real duty assigned to his true self; and hence it is also injustice (*ẓulm*) to the self. It is tenacious adherence to pre-Islamic beliefs and super-stitions, and obstinate pride and ideologization of one's own pre-Islamic cultural traditions; or it is also secularization.

We observed earlier that Western theologians have made a distinction which appears to them as significant between secularization and secularism, where secularism is a name denoting not a process, but a crystallization, as it were, of the process of secularization into a particular and distinct form, an ideology. They have also implied that every ism is ideology. This of course depends upon how the term 'ideo-logy' is understood and to what term the ism is suffixed. In the first instance, if ideology is taken to mean a set of general ideas, or philosophical program without having any reference to its interpretation and implementation as the worldview of a state, then so is secularization, as they have conceived it, an ideology; the distinction being that the worldview of one is 'closed' and that of the other is 'open'. If, however, ideology is taken to mean a set of general ideas, or philosophical program which finds expression as the official worldview of a state, then again, secularization, as they have conceived it, is also an ideology; for they have conceived secularization not merely as a historical process in which man is passively immersed, but that man himself is ever engaged actively in creating the process, so that in each generation man sets forth a philosophical program projecting a worldview officially adopted by the state even if that worldview should be in the form of a secular relativism. Secularization then, in the way they have conceived it, is not different from *secularizationism*. In the second instance, we say that not every ism is ideological in the second sense of the concept ideology as described above. Indeed it is the second sense of the concept ideology that we are in fact concerned with, since that is the sense they have in mind although they have not stated it definitely, for both secularism and secularization in the way they have conceived it almost as similar worldviews are worldviews applicable to state and society. So then in this sense, which is the sense they mean, we say that not every ism is ideological, for it depends upon the conceptual designation of the term to which it is suffixed. When ism is suffixed to secular, or capital, or social, or nihil, it denotes an ideology. But when ism is suffixed to real, or rational, it does not denote an ideology in this sense. Perhaps so in the first sense described above. Nevertheless we can conceive and speak of an Islamic rationalism, and not of an Islamic secularism; so as far as we are concerned the implications inherent in the second sense of the concept ideology, although undoubtedly derived from the first sense of it, deserves our immediate attention, for that is the sense in which secularism and secularization, or secularizationism pose an immediate threat to us. Irrespective of the academic distinction made between the 'open' worldview projected by secularizationism on the one hand, and the 'closed' worldview projected by secularism on the other, both are equally opposed to the worldview projected by Islam. As far as their opposition to Islām is concerned we do not find the distinction between them significant enough for us to justify our making a special distinction between them from the point of view of practical judgement. In fact, in spite of what those theologians say about secularization having its roots in biblical faith and secularism in Western philosophy and science — a claim which we have shown to be incorrect in that both have their roots in Western philosophy and science and metaphysics — the one might, according to the logic of historicity and 'evolution', indeed merge with the other. So in this book, therefore, and particularly with reference to its title: *Islām and Secularism*, the term secularism is meant to denote not merely secular ideologies such as, for example, Communism or Socialism in its various forms, but encompasses also all expressions of the secular worldview including that projected by secularization, which is none other than a secular historical relativism which I have called secularizationism.

We have said earlier that Christianity has no Revealed Law or *sharī'ah* such as we have in Islām, and this is because it was not really a revealed religion in the sense we understand. We also said that it has no clear concept of religion except in terms of faith vaguely expressed, and this fact is also related to what is said in the preceding sentence. Christian dogma develops, and has been developing since earliest times; it has always existed in a process of development. The realization that the religion develops is a recent discovery even among the theologians, and this is also perhaps why it has never been nor ever will be easy for them, in their experience and consciousness of existence, to define belief and faith and religion. Their secular authorities have indeed put forward what in fact amounts to *descriptions* of religion, which they ultimately reduce to a system of doctrines and pledges and rites which they understand to have 'developed' and 'evolved' with man as part of the historical process and the 'maturing' of man. The deeper aspects of religion are dealt with and interpreted not by theology, but by a new science which they have developed for that purpose called the Philosophy of Religion. The word *religion* itself, derived from Middle English *religioun*, from Old French *religion*, from Latin *religio*, which vaguely refers to a 'bond between man and the gods', does not yield much information about its meaning as a real and fundamental aspect of human life. Moreover, the idea of a covenant vaguely discerned behind the 'bond' existing between man and the gods has, because of the peculiar structure of the language, become confusingly opaque when applied to refer to the Universal God of true religion. No doubt there is general agreement among mankind that the concept of religion has to do with a kind of bond, but this is not clearly explained in the various religions, and no revealed Book of the People of the Book made any reference to any fundamental and original covenant between man and God. Only in the Holy Qur'ān is there found clear reference to this most important basis of religion, as will be shown in the next chapter.

III

ISLAM: THE CONCEPT OF RELIGION AND THE FOUNDATION OF ETHICS AND MORALITY

The concept couched in the term *dīn*, which is generally understood to mean *religion*, is not the same as the concept *religion* as interpreted and understood throughout Western religious history. When we speak of Islām and refer to it in English as a 'religion', we mean and understand by it the *dīn*, in which all the basic connotations inherent in the term *dīn*[40] are conceived as gathered into a single unity of coherent meaning as reflected in the Holy Qur'ān and in the Arabic language to which it belongs.

The word *dīn* derived from the Arabic root DYN has many primary significations which although seemingly contrary to one another are yet all conceptually interconnected, so that the ultimate meaning derived from them all presents itself as a clarified unity of the whole. By 'the whole' I mean that which is described as the Religion of Islām, which contains within itself all the relevant possi-

---

40 In this chapter my interpretation of the basic connotations inherent in the term *dīn* is based on Ibn Manẓur's standard classic, the *Lisān al-'Arab* (Beyrouth, 1968, 15v.), hereafter cited as *LA*. For what is stated in this page and the next, see vol. 13: 166, col. 2-171, col. 2.

bilities of meaning inherent in the concept of *dīn*. Since we are dealing with an Islamic concept which is translated into reality intimately and profoundly *lived* in human experience, the apparent contrariness in its basic meanings is indeed not due to vagueness; it is, rather, due to the contrariness inherent in human nature itself, which they faithfully reflect. And their power to reflect human nature faithfully is itself clear demonstration of their lucidity and veracity and authenticity in conveying truth.

The primary significations of the term *dīn* can be reduced to four: (1) *indebtedness*; (2) *submissiveness*; (3) *judicious power*; (4) *natural inclination* or *tendency*. In what presently follows, I shall attempt to explain them briefly and place them in their relevant contexts, drawing forth the coherent ultimate meaning intended, which denotes the faith, beliefs and practices and teachings adhered to by the Muslims individually and collectively as a Community and manifesting itself altogether as an objective whole as the Religion called *Islām*.

The verb *dāna* which derives from *dīn* conveys the meaning of *being indebted*, including various other meanings connected with *debts*, some of them contraries. In the state in which one finds oneself being in debt — that is to say, a *dā'in* — it follows that one subjects oneself, in the sense of *yielding* and *obeying*, to law and ordinances governing debts, and also, in a way, to the creditor, who is likewise designated as a *dā'in*.[41] There is also conveyed in the situation described the fact that one in debt is under *obligation*, or *dayn*. Being in debt and under obligation naturally involves *judgement: daynūnah*, and *conviction: idānah*, as the case may be. All the above significations including their contraries inherent in *dāna* are practicable possibilities only in

---

41 *Dā'in* refers both to *debtor* as well as *creditor*, and this apparent contrariness in meaning can indeed be resolved if we transpose both these meanings to refer to the two natures of man, that is, the rational soul and the animal or carnal soul. See below pp. 67-70.

organized societies involved in commercial life in *towns* and *cities*, denoted by *mudun* or *madā'in*. A town or city, a *madīnah*, has a *judge, ruler,* or *governor* — a *dayyān*. Thus already here, in the various applications of the verb *dāna* alone, we see rising before our mind's eye a picture of civilized living; of societal life of law and order and justice and authority.[42] It is, conceptually at least, connected intimately with another verb *maddana*[43] which means: to

---

42 It is I think extremely important to discern both the intimate and profoundly significant connection between the concept of *dīn* and that of *madīnah* which derives from it, and the role of the Believers individually in relation to the former and collectively in relation to the latter.

Considerable relevance must be seen in the significance of the change of name of the town once known as Yathrib to *al-Madīnah: the City* — or more precisely, *Madīnatu'l-Nabiy: the City of the Prophet* — which occurred soon after the Holy Prophet (may God bless and give him Peace!) made his historic Flight (*hijrah*) and settled there. The first Community of Believers was formed there at the time, and its was that Flight that marked the New Era in the history of mankind. We must see the fact that al-Madīnah was so called and named because it was there that true *dīn* became realised for mankind. There the Believers enslaved themselves under the authority and jurisdiction of the Holy Prophet (may God bless and give him Peace!), its *dayyān*; there the realization of the debt to God took definite form, and the approved manner and method of its repayment began to unfold. The City of the Prophet signified the Place where true *dīn* was enacted under his authority and jurisdiction. We may further see that the City became, for the Community, the epitome of the socio-political order of Islām; and for the individual Believer it became, by analogy , the symbol of the Believer's body and physical being in which the rational soul, in emulation of him who may God bless and give Peace!, exercises authority and just government. For further relevant interpretations, see below, pp. 54-63; 64-70; 71-79; 82-83.

43 *LA*, vol. 13:402,col. 2-403,col.1.

build or to *found cities*: to *civilize*, to *refine* and to *humanize*, from which is derived another term: *tamaddun*, meaning *civilization* and *refinement* in *social culture*. Thus we derive from the primary signification of being in a state of debt other correlated significations, such as: to *abase oneself*, to *serve* (a master), to *become enslaved*; and from another such signification of *judge*, *ruler* and *governor* is derived meanings which denote the *becoming mighty*, *powerful* and *strong*, *a master*, one *elevated in rank*, and *glorious*; and yet further, the meanings: *judgement*, *requital* or *reckoning* (at some appointed time). Now the very notion of law and order and justice and authority and social cultural refinement inherent in all these significations derived from the concept *dīn* must surely presuppose the existence of a *mode* or *manner of acting* consistent with what is reflected in the law, the order, the justice, the authority and social cultural refinement — a mode or manner of acting, or a *state of being* considered as *normal* in relation to them; so that this *state of being* is a state that is *customary* or *habitual*. From here, then, we can see the logic behind the derivation of the other primary signification of the concept *dīn* as *custom, habit, disposition* or *natural tendency*. At this juncture it becomes increasingly clear that the concept *dīn* in its most basic form indeed reflects in true testimony the natural tendency of man to form societies and obey laws and seek just government. The idea of a *kingdom*, a *cosmopolis*, inherent in the concept *dīn* that rises before our vision is most important in helping us attain a more profound understanding of it, and needs be reiterated here, for we shall have recourse to it again when we deal with the religious and spiritual aspects of man's existential experience.

I have thus far explained only in cursory manner the basic concept of *dīn*, reducing the various connotations to four primary significations and showing their mutual actual and primary conceptual connections, in the context of human 'secular' relations. In the religious context, that of the relationship between man and God, and what God approves of man's relations with his fellow-men, the primary significations, while maintaining their basic meanings, nevertheless undergo profound synthesis and intensification at once true to the experience described and to the description of the Religion of Islām as the objective faith, beliefs and practices and teachings experienced and lived by each and every member of the Muslim Community as well as by the Community as a whole.

How can the concept of *being indebted* be explained in the religious and spiritual context? — one may ask; what is the nature of the debt?, and to whom is the debt owed? We answer that man is indebted to God, his Creator and Provider, for bringing him into existence and maintaining him in his existence. Man was once nothing and did not exist, and now he is:

ولقد خلقنا الانسان من سللة من طين

ثم جعلنه نطفة في قرار مكين

ثم خلقنا النطفة علقة وخلقنا العلقة مضغة

وخلقنا المضغة عظما فكسونا العظم لحما

ثم انشانه خلقا اخر

فتبرك الله احسن الخالقين

Man We did create from a quintessence of clay;
Then We placed him as a drop of sperm in a place of rest, firmly fixed;
Then We made the sperm into a clot of congealed blood; then of that clot We made a lump; then We made out of that lump bones and clothed the bones with flesh; then We developed out of it another creature. So blessed be God, the Best to create!'[44]

The man who ponders seriously his origin will realize that a few decades ago he did not exist, and the whole of mankind now existing neither existed nor knew of their possible present existence. The same truth applies to all ages of man from the beginnings of his existence in time.

---

44 *Al-Mu'minūn* (23):12-14.

So naturally he who ponders thus sincerely knows intuitively that his sense of being indebted for his creation and existence cannot really be directed to his parents, for he knows equally well that his parents too are subject to the same process by the same Creator and Provider. Man does not himself cause his own growth and development from the state of a clot of congealed blood to the one that now stands mature and perfect. He knows that even in his mature and perfect state he is not able to create for himself his sense of sight or hearing or other — and let alone move himself in conscious growth and development in his helpless embryonic stage. Then again:

واذ ا خذ ربك من بني ادم

من ظهورهم ذريتهم واشهدهم

على انفسهم الست بربكم

قالوا بلى شهدنا

'When thy Lord drew forth from the Children of Ādam — from their loins — their descendents, and made them testify concerning themselves (saying): "Am I not your Lord?" — they said:"Yea! we do testify!"[45]

The rightly guided man realizes that his very self, his soul, has already acknowledged God as his Lord, even before his existence as a man, so that such a man recognizes his Creator and Cherisher and Sustainer. The nature of the debt of creation and existence is so tremendously total that man, the moment he is created and given existence, is already in a state of utter loss, for he possesses really nothing himself, seeing that everything about him and in him and from him is what the Creator owns Who owns everything. And this is the purport of the words in the Holy Qur'ān:

---

45 *Al-A'rāf*(7):172.

ان الانسان لفي خسر

'Verily man is in loss (*khusrin*)'.[46]

Seeing that he owns absolutely nothing to 'repay' his debt, *except his own consciousness* of the fact *that he is himself the very substance* of the debt, so must he 'repay' with himself, so must he 'return' himself to Him Who owns him absolutely. He is himself the debt to be returned to the Owner, and 'returning the debt' means to *give himself up in service*, or *khidmah*, to his Lord and Master; to *abase himself* before Him — and so the rightly guided man sincerely and consciously *enslaves himself* for the sake of God in order to fulfill His Commands and Prohibitions and Ordinances, and thus to live out the dictates of His Law. The concept of 'return' alluded to above is also evident in the conceptual structure of *dīn,*for it can and does indeed mean, as I will elaborate in due course, a 'return to man's inherent nature', the concept 'nature' referring to the spiritual and not altogether the physical aspect of man's being.[47] It must also be pointed out that in the words of the Holy Qur'ān:

والسماء ذات االرجع

---

46 *Al-'Aṣri*(103):2.

47 The concept of return is also expressed in the meaning of the term '*uwwida* in the sense of returning to the past, that is, to tradition. Hence the signification of *dīn* as custom or habit. In this sense it means return to the tradition of the Prophet Ibrāhīm (upon whom be Peace!). In this connection please see above p.54 and below, pp. 61-65. It must be pointed out that by 'tradition' here is not meant the kind of tradition that originated and evolved in human history and culture and had its source in the human mind. It is rather, what God has revealed and commanded and taught His Prophets and Messengers, so that although they appeared in successive and yet unconnected periods in history, they conveyed and acted as if what they conveyed and acted upon had been embodied in the continuity of a tradition.

'By the heaven that hath rain'.[48]

the word interpreted as 'rain' is *raj'*, which means literally 'return'.[49] It is interpreted as rain because God returns it time and again, and it refers to good return in the sense of *benefit, profit,* and *gain. Raj'* is therefore used synonymously in this sense with *rabaḥ,* meaning gain,[50] which is the opposite or contrary of *khusr,* loss, to which reference has already been made above. Now it is appropriate to mention here that one of the basic meanings of *dīn* which has not been explained above is recurrent rain, rain that returns again and again; and hence we perceive that *dīn* here, like such a rain, alludes to benefit and gain (*rabaḥ*). When we say that in order to 'repay' his debt man must 'return' himself to God, his Owner, his 'returning himself' is, like the returning rain,[51] a gain unto him. And this is the meaning of the saying:

من دان نفسه ربح

'He who enslaves himself gains (*rabiḥa* whose infinitive noun is: *rabaḥ*).'[52]

The expression 'enslaves himself' (*dāna nafsahu*) means 'gives himself up' (in service), and hence also 'returns himself' (to his Owner) as explained.[53] The same meaning

---

48 *Al-Ṭāriq*(86):II; *LA*, vol. 8:120, col.2.

49 There is a close connection between the concept here described and the application of the verb *raja'a* in its various forms in the Holy Qur'ān with reference to man's return to God.

50 *LA*, vol. 2:442, col. 2–445, col. 1.

51 True *dīn* brings life to a body otherwise dead just as 'the rain which God sends down from the skies, and the life which he gives therewith to an earth that is dead.' See *al-Baqarah*(2):164.

52 *LA*, vol. 13:1667, col. 1.

53 It clearly refers to the man who, having consciously realized that he is himself the subject of his own debt to His Creator and Sustainer and Cherisher, enslaves himself to his self and hence 'returns' himself to his true Lord.

is expressed in the words of the Holy Prophet, may God bless and give him Peace!:

الكيس من دان نفسه

وعمل لما بعدالموت

"The intelligent one is he who enslaves himself (*dāna nafsahu*) and works for that which shall be after death."[54]

'That which shall be after death' is that which shall be reckoned good, the requital, the good return. This good return is like the returning rain which brings benefit to the earth by bringing life to it and by causing goodly growth beneficial to life to grow from it. In like manner that rain gives life to the earth which would otherwise be dead, so does *dīn* give life to man, without which man would be as one who is, as it were, also 'dead'. This is aptly symbolized by God's Words in the Holy Qur'ān, where He says:

وما انزل الله من السمأ

من مأ فاحيابه الارض بعد موتها

...In the rain which God sends down from the skies, and the life which He gives therewith to an earth that is dead — [55]

By returning himself' to his Lord and Master, by loyally and truly following and obeying God's Commands and Prohibitions and Ordinances and Law, the man thus acting will be requited and will receive his good return multiplied many times over, as God says in the Holy Qur'ān:

من ذالذي يقرض الله قرضا حسنا

فيضعفه له اضعا فا كثيرة

---

54 *LA*, vol. 13:169, col. 2.
55 *Al-Baqarah* (2):164

'Who is he who will loan (*yuqriḍu*) to God a beautiful loan (*qarḍan ḥasanan*) which God will double to his credit and multiply many times?[56]

Notice here that the verb used to signify 'loan' (*yuqriḍu*), from *qaraḍa, qarḍ* has not the same connotation as that which is termed as 'debt' (*dayn*), for the latter term is applicable to man only. The 'loan' here meant is 'the return of that which is owned 'originally' by the One Who now asks for it, and which is to be returned to Him.' Man is God;'s property and his existence is only 'lent' him for a time. On the other hand the expression 'goodly loan' (*qarḍan ḥasanan*) as applied to man has a metaphorical significance, in that it is his 'service to God', his 'good works' that is meant, for these can indeed be said to *belong* to him, and for the offering of which he will be requited in abundance. God is the Requiter, the Supreme Judge: *al-dayyān*. He is the King, *mālik*, of the Day of Judgement and Requital, *yawm al-dīn*, also called the Day of Reckoning, *yawm al-ḥisāb*.[57] The fact that God is referred to as King, and everything else as the Kingdom over which He exercises Absolute Power and Authority, *malakūt*, shows again that man is His *mamlūk*, His slave. So *dīn* in the religious context also refers to the state of being a slave.[58] We referred a while ago to man's 'returning himself' as meaning 'giving himself up in service' (*khidmah*) to God. We now say that in effect what is truly meant is not 'service' in the sense of *any* service, or the kind offered to another man or human institution. The concept of *khidmah* implies that the one

---

56 *Al-Baqarah* (2):245.

57 *Dīn* also means correct reckoning: *ḥisāb al-ṣaḥīḥ*. It is the apportioning of the precisely correct measure to a number or thing so that it fits into its proper place: *'adad al-mustawā*. This somewhat mathematical meaning conveys the sense of there being a system or law governing all and maintaining all in perfect equilibrium. See *LA.* vol. 13:169, col. 1.

58 *LA*, vol. 13:170, col. 1.

who gives such service is 'free', is not a bondman, but is 'his own master' in respect of himself. The concept *mamlūk*, however, conveys the implicit fact of ownership by the one who takes his service. The *mamlūk* is possessed by the *mālik*. So we do not say of one who serves God that he is a *khādim*, meaning servant, but that he is God's *'ābid*, and he is in truth God's *'abd*, meaning also servant or slave, which term has the connotation of 'being owned' by Him Whom he serves. In the religious context, therefore, *'abd* is the correct term of reference to one who, in the realization that he is indebted absolutely to God, abases himself in service to Him; and hence the act of service appropriate for him is called *'ibādah* and the service is *'ibādāt*, which refers to all conscious and willing acts of service for the sake of God alone and approved by Him, including such as are prescribed worship. By worshipping God in such manner of service the man is fulfilling the purpose for his creation and existence, as God says in the Holy Qur'ān:

وما خلقت الجن والا نس الا ليعبدون

'I have only created the Jinn and Man that they may serve Me' (*ya 'budūni*).[59]

When we say that such a man is fulfilling the purpose for his creation and existence, it is obvious that that man's obligation to serve God is felt by him as *normal* because it comes as a *natural inclination* on the man's part to do so. This natural tendency in the man to serve and worship God is also referred to as *dīn*, as we have observed in the beginning in connection with its connotation as *custom, habit,* and *disposition.* However, here in the religious context is has a more specific signification of the *natural state of being* called *fiṭrah*. In fact *dīn* does also mean *fiṭrah*.[60] *Fiṭrah* is the pattern according to which God has created all things.

---

59 *Al-Dhāriyāt*(51):56.
60 *LA*,vol. 5:58, cols. 1 & 2; see also *al-Rūm*(30):30.

It is God's manner of creating, *sunnat Allāh*, and everything fits each into its pattern created for it and set in its proper place. It is the Law of God. Submission to it brings harmony, for it means realization of what is inherent in one's true nature; opposition to it brings discord, for it means realization of what is extraneous to one's true nature. It is *cosmos* as opposed to *chaos*; justice as opposed to injustice. When God said:"Am I not your Lord?", and man's true self, testifying for itself, answered:"Yea!" in acknowledgement of the truth of God's Lordship, it has sealed a Covenant with God. Thus when man is manifested as man in this wordly life he will, if rightly guided, remember his Covenant and act accordingly as outlined above, so that his worship, his acts of piety, his life and death is lived out for the sake of God alone. One of the meanings of *fiṭrah* as *dīn* refers to the realization of this Covenant by man.[61] Submission in the sense described above means *conscious, willing* submission, and this submission does not entail loss of 'freedom' for him, since freedom in fact means *to act as his true nature demands*. The man who submits to God in this way is living out the *dīn*.

Submission, we say again, refers to conscious and willing submission, for were it neither conscious nor willing it cannot then mean *real* submission. The concept of submission is perhaps common to all religions, just as belief or faith is the core of all religions, but we maintain that not all religions enact real submission. Neither is the submission meant the kind that is momentary or erratic, for real submission is a continuous act lived throughout the entire span of one's ethical life; nor is it the kind that operates only within the realm of the heart without manifesting itself outwardly in the action of the body as works performed in obedience to God's Law. Submission to God's Will means also obedience to His Law. The word denoting this sense of submission is *aslama*, as is evident in

---

61   *LA*, vol. 5:56, col. 2, 57, col. 1.

the Holy Qur'ān where God says:

ومن احسن دينا ممن اسلم وجهه لله

Who can be better in religion (*dīn*) than one who submits (*aslama*) his face (i.e., his whole self) to God...[62]

The *dīn* referred to is none other than Islām. There are, no doubt, other forms of *dīn*, but the one in which is enacted total submission (*istislām*) to God alone is the best, and this one is the only *dīn* acceptable to God, as He says in the Holy Qur'ān:

ومن يبتغ غيرالاسلام دينا فلن يقبل منه

If anyone desires a religion (*dīn*) other than Islām (*al-Islām*), never will it be accepted of him...[63]

and again:

ان الدين عندالله الاسلام

Verily the Religion (*al-dīn*) in the sight of God is Islām (*al-Islām*).[64]

According to the Holy Qur'ān, man cannot escape being in the state of living a *dīn* since all submit (*aslama*) to God's will. Hence the term *dīn* is also used to denote religions other than Islām. However, what makes Islām different from the other religions is that the submission according to Islām is *sincere* and *total* submission to God's Will, and this is enacted *willingly* as absolute obedience to the Law revealed by Him. This idea is implicitly expressed in the Holy Qur'ān, for example, in the following passage:

افغيردين الله يبغون وله اسلم

---

62 *Al-Nisā'* (4):125.
63 *Āli 'Imrān* (3):85.
64 *Āli 'Imrān* (3):19.x

63

من في السموت والارض طوعاو

كرها واليه يرجعون

Do they seek or other than the religion (*dīn*) of God?
while all creatures in the heavens and on earth have,
willing or unwilling, submitted (*aslama*) to His Will, and
to Him shall they all be returned.[65]

The form in which submission is enacted or expressed is
the form of the *dīn*, and it is here that diversity occurs
between one *dīn* and another.[66] This form, which is the
manner of institution of belief and faith, the manner of
expression of the law, the manner of religious attitude and
ethical and moral conduct — the manner in which
submission to God is enacted in our life, is expressed by the
concept *millah*. Islām follows the *millah* of the Prophet
Ibrāhīm (Abraham), which is also the *millah* of the other
Prophets after him (Peace be upon them all!). Their *millah*
altogether is considered to be the form of the right religion
dīn al-qayyim, because of all other *milal*, their *millah* alone
inclined perfectly, *ḥanīfan*, towards the true Religion (al-
Islām). They thus anticipate Islām in religious faith and
belief and law and practice and hence are called also
Muslims, even though the Religion of Islām as such
reached its perfect crystallization only in the form
externalized by the Holy Prophet (may God bless and give
him Peace!). Other religions have evolved their own
systems or forms of submission based upon their own
cultural traditions which do not necessarily derive from the

---

65 *Āli 'Imrān* (3):83.

66 This of course does not imply that the diversity between
religions is only a matter of form, for the difference in the
form indeed implies a difference in the conception of God,
His Essence and Attributes and Names and Acts — a
difference in the conception expressed in Islām as *tawḥīd*: the
Unity of God.

millah of the Prophet Ibrāhīm (upon whom be Peace!) and yet some others, such as the *dīn* of the *Ahlu'l-Kitāb* — People of the Book — have evolved a mixture of their own cultural traditions with traditions based upon Revelation. It is to these various systems or forms of submission that, to return to the passage just quoted, the "unwilling" type of submission refers.[67]

---

67 In a sense, the words of God in the Holy Qur'ān:

لا اكره في الدين

   — Let there be no compulsion in religion (*al-Baqarah* (2):256) — corroborates what has been explained above in that in true religion there should be no compulsion: not only in the sense that, in the act of subjugating to religion and submitting to it, one must not compel others to submit; but in the sense that even with oneself, one must subjugate and submit oneself wholeheartedly and willingly, and love and enjoy the submission. Unwilling submission betrays arrogance, disobedience and rebellion, and is tantamount to misbelief, which is one of the forms of unbelief (*kufr*). It is a mistake to think belief in One God alone is sufficient in true religion, and that such belief guarantees security and salvation. Iblīs (Satan), who believes in the One True God and knows and acknowledges Him as his Creator, Cherisher and Sustainer, his *rabb*, is nevertheless a misbeliever (*kāfir*). Although Iblīs submits to God, yet he submits grudgingly and insolently, and his *kufr* is due to arrogance, disobedience and rebellion, His is the most notorious example of unwilling submission. Unwilling submission, then, is not the mark of true belief, and a *kāfir* might therefore be also one who, though professing belief in One God, does not submit in real submission, but prefers instead to submit in his own obstinate way — a way, or manner, or form neither approved nor revealed and commanded by God. Real submission is that which has been perfected by the Holy Prophet (may God bless and give him Peace!) as the model for mankind, for that is the manner of submission of all the Prophets and Messengers before him, and the form approved, revealed, and commanded by God. Thus, the fundamental core of true

The concept of *dīn* in the sense of true obedience and real submission such as is here described in brief outline is manifested in living reality in the Religion of Islām. It is in Islām that true and perfect *dīn* is realized, for in Islām alone is its self-expression fulfilled completely. Islām emulates the pattern or form according to which God governs His Kingdom; it is an imitation of the cosmic order manifested here in this worldly life as a social as well as political order. The social order of Islām encompasses all aspects of man's physical and material and spiritual existence in a way which, here and now, does justice to the individual as well as the society; and to the individual as a physical being as well as the individual as spirit, so that a Muslim is at once himself and his Community, and his Community is also he, since every other single member strives, like him, to realize the same purpose in life and to achieve the same goal. The social order of Islām is the Kingdom of God on earth, for in that order God, and not man, is *still* the King, the Supreme Sovereign Whose Will and Law and Ordinances and Commands and Prohibitions hold absolute sway. Man is only His vicegerent or *khalīfah*, who is given the trust of government, the *amānah*, to rule according to God's Will and His Pleasure. When we say "rule", we do not simply mean to refer to the socio-political sense of 'ruling', for we mean by it also — indeed far more fundamentally so — the ruling of one's self by itself, since the trust refers to responsibility and freedom of the self to do justice to itself. Of this last statement we shall have recourse to elaborate presently, since what is meant reveals the very principle of Islamic ethics and morality. Islām, we say again, is a social order, but in that order every individual, each according to his latent capacity and power bestowed upon him by God to fulfill and realize his responsibility and freedom, strives to achieve and realize

---

religion, then, is not the *belief*, but rather , more fundamentally, the submission; for the *submission* confirms and affirms the *belief* to be true and genuine.

the ideal for himself in the Way[68] manifested by the Revealed Law[69] obeyed by all members of the Community. Thus then, just as every Muslim is a *khalīfah* of God on earth, so is every Muslim also His slave, His *'abd*, striving by himself to perfect his service and devotion, his *'ibādah*, in the manner approved by God, his Absolute Master. And since every individual in this social order is answerable to God alone, so even in that social order each individual is personally directing his true and real loyalty, *ṭā'ah*, to God alone, his Real King.

We have already said that the concept *dīn* reflects the idea of a kingdom — a cosmopolis. Commerce and trade are the life blood of the cosmopolis, and such activity together with its various implications is indeed inherent in the concept *dīn* as we have thus far described. It is no wonder then that in the Holy Qur'ān worldly life is depicted so persistently in the apt metaphors of commercial enterprise. In the cosmopolis or kingdom reflected in the concept *dīn*, there is depicted the bustling activities of the traffic of trade. Man is inexorably engage in the trade: *al-tijārah*, in which he is himself the subject as well as object of this trade. He is his own capital, and his loss and gain depend upon his own sense of responsibility and exercise of freedom. He carries out the trust of buying and selling, of *bay'ah*, and bartering: *ishtarā*; and it is his self that he buys or sells or barters; and depending upon his own inclination towards the exercise of his will and deeds his trade will either prosper: *rabiḥa'l-tijārah*, or suffer loss: *mā rabiḥa'l-tijārah*. In the situation that rises before our vision we must see that the man so engaged realizes the utter seriousness of the trading venture he has willingly undertaken.[70] He is not simply an animal that eats and

---

68 By 'the Way' I mean what refers to *iḥsān*, or perfection in virtue.

69 The Revealed Law, or *sharī'ah*, is the Law of God.

70 See *al-Aḥzāb* (33):72.

drinks and sleeps and disports after sensual pleasure[71] — no
savage nor barbarian he who thus transcends himself in the
realization of his weighty responsibility and consciousness
of his freedom to fulfill and redeem himself of the burden
of existence. It is of such as he who barters his self for his
true self that God refers when He says in the Holy Qur'ān:

ان الله اشترى من المؤمنين انفسهم

Verily God has purchased of the Believers their
selves — .[72]

The concept *dīn* with reference to the man of Islām[73] pre-
supposes the emergence in him of the higher type of man
capable of lofty aspirations towards self-improvement — the
self-improvement that is no less than the actualization of his
latent power and capacity to become a perfect man. The
man of Islām as a city dweller, a cosmopolitan, living a
civilized life according to clearly defined foundations of
social order and codes of conduct is he to whom obedience
to Divine Law, endeavour towards realizing true justice and
striving after right knowledge are cardinal virtues. The
motive of conduct of such a man is eternal blessedness,
entrance into a state of supreme peace which he might
even here perchance foretaste, but which shall be vouchsafed to him when he enters the threshold of that other
City and becomes a dweller, a citizen of that other Kingdom
wherein his ultimate bliss shall be the beholding of the
Glorious Countenance of the King.

While Islām is the epitome of the Divine cosmic order,
the man of Islām who is conscious of his destiny realizes
that he is himself, as physical being, also an epitome of the
cosmos, a microcosmic representation, *'ālam saghīr*, of the
Macrocosmos, *al-'ālam al-kabīr*. Hence in the manner that
Islām is like a kingdom, a social order, so the man of Islām

---

71 See *al-A'rāf* (7):179.   72 *Al-Tawbah* (9):111.
73 The man of Islām, *i.e.*, the Muslim.

knows that he is a kingdom in miniature, for in him, as in all mankind, is manifested the Attributes of the Creator, without the reverse being the case, since "God created man in His Own Image." Now man is both soul and body, he is at once physical being and spirit, and his soul governs his body as God governs the Universe. Man also has two souls analogous to his dual nature: the higher, rational soul: *al-nafs al-nāṭiqah*; and the lower, animal or carnal soul: *al-nafs al-ḥayawāniyyah*. Within the conceptual framework of the concept *dīn* applied here as a subjective, personal, individual affair, man's rational soul is king and must exert its power and rule over the animal soul which is subject to it and which must be rendered submissive to it. The effective power and rule exercised by the rational soul over the animal soul and the subjugation and total submission of the latter to the former can indeed be interpreted as *dīn*, or as *islām* in the subjective, personal, individual sense of the relationship thus established. In this context it is the animal soul that enslaves itself in submission and service and so 'returns' itself to the power and authority of the rational soul. When the Holy Prophet (may God bless and give him Peace!) said:

موتوا قبل ان تموتوا

"Die before ye die." —

it is the same as saying : "Return before ye *actually* return"; and this refers to the subjugation of one's self by one's real self, one's animal soul by one's rational soul; and it is pertaining to knowledge of this Self that he means when he says:

من عرف نفسه فقد عرف ربه

"He who knows his Self knows his Lord"

Further, when God proclaimed His Lordship to Ādam's progeny it is the rational soul of man that He addressed, so

69

that every soul has heard the "Am I not your Lord?" and answered "Yea!" and testified thus unto itself. So the man of Islām who is rightly guided acts accordingly as befits the true servant of God, His *'abd.* We referred earlier to the purpose for man's creation and existence, saying that it is to serve God; and we said that the act of service on the man's part is called *'ibādah* and the service as such *'ibādāt,* which refers to all conscious and willing acts of service for the sake of God alone and approved by Him, including such as are prescribed worship. In point of fact, we now say further that to the man of Islām his whole ethical life is one continuous *'ibādah,* for Islām itself is a complete way of life. When the man has, by means of *'ibādāt,* succeeded in curbing his animal and carnal passions and has thereby rendered submissive his animal soul, making it subject to the rational soul, the man thus described has attained to freedom in that he has fulfilled the purpose for his creation and existence; he has achieved supreme peace[74] and his soul is pacified, being set at liberty, as it were, free from the fetters of inexorable fate and the noisy strife and hell of human vices. His rational soul in this spiritual station is called in the Holy Qur'ān the 'pacified' or tranquil' soul: *al-nafs al-muṭma' innah.* This is the soul that 'returns' itself willingly to its Lord, and to it will God address His Words:

ياايتها النفس المطمئنة ارجعى الى ربك

راضية مرضية فادخلى في عبدى وادخلى جنتى

"O thou soul at peace! Return thou to thy Lord, — well-pleased (thyself) and well-pleasing unto Him! Enter thou, then, among My servants! Yea, enter thou My Heaven!"[75]

---

74 When we also say that Islām means 'Peace', we refer in fact to the consequence of the submission denoted by the verb *aslama.*

75 *Al Fajr* (89):27-30.

This is the soul of the servant who has fulfilled in constant affirmation his Covenant with his Lord, and since none *knows* his Lord better than the true and loyal servant, who by reason of such service gains *intimacy* with his Lord and Master, so *'ibādah* means, in its final, advanced stages, knowledge: *ma'rifah.*[76]

I have traced in bare outline the fundamental core of the Religion of Islām and have shown in a general way which can, albeit, be elaborated to its minutest logical details its all-encompassing nature which pervades the life of the individual as well as the society. I have said that Islām is the subjective, personal religion of the individual as well as the objective, pervading self-same religion of the Community — that it operates as the same religion in the individual as a

---

76 We do not in the least imply here that when *'ibādah* becomes identified with *ma'rifah*, the former as work or service (*'amal*) including prayer (*ṣalāt*) — i.e. the prescribed (*farḍ*), the confirmed practice of the Prophet (*sunnah*), the super-erogatory (*nawāfil*) — is no longer incumbent on the one who attains to the latter, or that for such a one prayer means simply intellectual contemplation, as some philosophers thought. *Ma'rifah* as 'knowledge' is both right cognition (*'ilm*) and right feeling or spiritual mood (*ḥāl*); and the former, which marks the final stages of the spiritual 'stations' (*maqāmāt*), precedes the latter, which marks the beginning of the spiritual 'states' (*aḥwāl*). So *ma'rifah* marks the spiritual transition-point between the spiritual station and the spiritual state. As such, and since it is knowledge that comes form God to the heart (*qalb*) and depends entirely upon Him, it is not necessarily a permanent condition unless continually secured and fortified by *'ibādah.* He who discerns knows that it is absurd in the case of one who receives knowledge from God about God (*i.e.* the *'ārif*) to transform thereby his *'ibadah* solely into contemplation, for the *'ārif* is acutely aware of the fact that he becomes one at least partly due to his *'ibādah,* which is the means by which he approaches his Lord.

single entity as well as the society composed collectively of such entities.[77] It is implicit in our exposition that Islām is both belief and faith (*īmān*) as well as submission in service (*islām*); it is both assent of the heart (*qalb*) and mind (*'aql*) confirmed by the tongue (*lisān*) as well as deed and work (*'amal*);[78] it is the harmonious relationship established between both the soul and the body; it is obedience and loyalty (*ṭā'ah*) both to God as well as to the Holy Prophet (may God bless and give him Peace!); it is accepting whole-heartedly the truth of the Testimony (*kalimah shahādah*) that there is no God but Allāh, and that Muḥammad is the Messenger of Allāh — Islām is the unity of all these, together with what they entail, in belief and in practice, in the person of the Muslim as well as in the Community as a whole. There can be no separation, nor division, nor dichotomy between the harmoniously integrated parts of the unity thus established so that there can be, for Islām, no

---

77 There is in truth no such thing as subjective Islām and objective Islām in the sense that the former implies less of its reality and truth than the latter, to the extent that the former is regarded as less valid and less authentic than the latter; or that the latter is other than the former as one independent reality and truth while the former is the many interpretations of the experience of the latter. We maintain that what is experienced as Islām by every individual Muslim subjectively is the same as Islām as it objectively is, and we use the terms 'subjective' and 'objective' here to distinguish rather than to differentiate the one form the other. The distinction between the two pertains to the level of understanding and the degree of insight and practice existing between one Muslim and another. The distinction thus refers to the *iḥsān-* aspect of Islamic experience. In spite of the naturally different levels of understanding and degrees of insight and practice existing between one Muslim and another yet all are Muslims and there is only one Islam, and what is common to them all is the same Islām.

78 *I.e.,* '*ibādah* and acts of '*ibādāt.*

true believer nor faithful one (*Mu'min*) without such a one being also submissive in service (*Muslim*); no real assent of heart and mind confirmed by tongue without deed and work; no genuine obedience and loyalty to God without obedience and loyalty to His Messenger; nor can there be true acceptance of the Testimony that there is no God but Allāh without also accepting Muḥammad as His Messenger, who in fact first made manifest the Formula of Unity (*kalimah al-tawḥīd*). I have also pointed out the fundamental nature of the Quranic revelation of the soul's Covenant with God in respect of His Lordship and the concept of *dīn* as reflecting the cosmos, as God's government of the realm of Creation, and I have drawn a comparison in respect of that concept of *dīn* and the concept of the macrocosm and its analogous relationship with man as a microcosm in which his rational soul governs his animal soul and body as God governs His Kingdom. The soul's Covenant with God and the nature of the relationship revealed in that Covenant indeed occupies a central position in the concept of *dīn* and is the fundamental basis of Islām, as I will reveal yet further. The Covenant was made to all souls of Ādam's progeny and God addressed them both collectively as well as individually, so that it was a covenant made at once by every individual soul as well as all of them collectively to acknowledge God as their Lord. To acknowledge God as Lord (*rabb*) means to acknowledge Him as Absolute King (syn. *mālik*), Possessor and Owner (syn. *ṣāḥib*), Ruler, Governor, Master, Creator, Cherisher, Sustainer — since all these meanings denote the connotations inherent in the concept of *Lord*. All souls have the same status in relation to their Lord: that of being subject, possessed, owned, ruled, governed, enslaved, created, cherished and sustained. And since the Covenant pertained at once to the individual soul as well as to the souls collectively, so we see that here when manifested as man within the fold of Islām the same souls are united in their endeavour to fulfill the Covenant collectively as society and Community (*ummah*) as well as individually in such wise that Islām is, as we have said, both personal and subjective as well as social and communal and objective,[79] it is the harmonious blending of both the individual as well as the society. That which unites one Muslim individual to another in a wondrous and unique bond of brotherhood which transcends the restricting limitations of race and nation and space and time and is much stronger than even the familial bond of kinship is none other than this Covenant, for those souls that here as man abide by that Covenant recognize each other as brothers, as kindred souls. They were akin to one another in yonder place and here they are brethren who love one another for God's sake. Though one be in the East and the other in the West, yet they feel joy and comfort in each other's talk, and one who lives in a later generation than the other is instructed and consoled by the words of his brother. They were brothers involved in the same destiny long before they appeared as earthly brothers, and they were true kith and kin before they were born in earthly kinship. So here we see that the same Covenant is the very basis of Islamic brotherhood (*ukhuwwah*). It is this real feeling of brotherhood among Muslims based upon such firm spiritual foundations which no earthly power can rend asunder that unite the individual to the society in Islām without the individual having to suffer loss of individuality and personality, nor the society its polity and authority.

In the Islamic political and social organization — be it in one form or another — the same Covenant becomes their very foundation. The man of Islām is not bound by the social contract, nor does he espouse the doctrine of the Social Contract. Indeed, though he lives and works within the bounds of social polity and authority and contributes his share towards the social good, and though he behaves *as if* a social contract were in force, his is, nevertheless, an *individual contract* reflecting the Covenant his soul has sealed with God; for the Covenant is in reality made *for each*

---

79 See above, note 77.

and every individual soul. The purpose and end of ethics in Islām is ultimately for the individual; what the man of Islām does here he does in the way he believes to be good only because God and His Messenger say so and he trusts that his actions will find favour with God. Neither the state nor the society are for him real and true objects of his loyalty and obedience, for to him they are not the prerogatives of state and society to the extent that such conduct is due to them as their right; and if he in an Islamic state and society lives and strives for the good of the state and the society, it is only because the society composed of individual men of Islām and the state organized by them set the same Islamic end and purpose as their goal — otherwise he is obliged to oppose the state and strive to correct the errant society and remind them of their true aim in life. We know that in the ultimate analysis man's quest for 'happiness' — as they say in philosophy in connection with ethics — is always for the individual self. It is not the 'happiness' of the collective entity that matters so much more than individual happiness; and every man in reality must indeed think and act for his own salvation, for no other man can be made responsible for his actions since every man bears his own burden of responsibility.[80] 'Happiness' refers not to the physical entity in man, not to the animal soul and body of man; nor is it a state of mind — it has to do with certainty of the ultimate Truth and fulfilment of action in conformity with that certainty; and certainty is a permanent condition referring to what is permanent in man and perceived by his spiritual organ known as the heart (*al-qalb*). It is peace and security and tranquility of the heart; it is knowledge, and knowledge is true belief; it is knowing one's rightful, and hence proper, place in the realm of Creation and one's proper relationship with the Creator; it is a condition known as *'adl* or justice.

In Islām — because for it religion encompasses life in its

---

80 See *al-Anʿām* (6):164.

entirety — all virtue is religious; it has to do with the freedom of the rational soul, which freedom means the power to do justice to itself; and this in turn refers to exercise of its rule and supremacy and guidance and maintenance over the animal soul and body. The power to do justice to itself alludes to its constant affirmation and fulfilment of the Covenant it has sealed with God. *Justice* in Islām is not a concept referring to a state of affairs which can operate only within a two-person-relation or dual-party-relation situation, such as: between one man and another; or between the society and the state; or between the ruler and the ruled; or between the king and his subjects. To the question: "Can one be unjust to one's self?" other religions or philosophies have not given a consistent clear-cut answer. Indeed in Western civilization, for example, though it is true that a man who commits suicide may be considered as committing an unjust act; but this is considered as such insofar only because his suicide deprives the state of the services of a useful citizen, so that his injustice is not to himself, but to the state and society. We have several times alluded to the concept that justice means a harmonious condition or state of affairs whereby every thing is in its right and proper place — such as the cosmos; or similarly, a state of equilibrium, whether it refers to things or living beings. With respect to man, we say that justice means basically a condition and situation whereby he is in his right and proper place. 'Place' here refers not only to his total situation in relation to others, but also to his condition in relation to his self. So the concept of justice in Islām does not only refer to relational situations of harmony and equilibrium existing between one person and another, or between the society and the state, or between the ruler and the ruled, or between the king and his subjects, but far more profoundly and fundamentally so it refers in a primary way to the harmonious and rightly-balanced relationship existing between the man and his self, and in a secondary way only to such as exists between him and another or others, between him and his fellow men and ruler and king and state and society. Thus to the question: "Can one be unjust to one's self?" we answer in the affirmative, and add further that justice and injustice indeed begins and ends with the self. The Holy Qur'ān repeatedly stresses the point that man, when he does wrong, is being unjust (ẓālim) to himself, and that injustice (ẓulm) is a condition wrought by man upon his self.[81] To understand this we have to refer once again to the soul's Covenant with God and to the belief that man has a dual nature in respect of his two souls and body. The real man can only in fact be his rational soul. If in his existence as a human being he allows his animal or carnal soul to get the better of him and consequently commits acts prohibited by God and displeasing to Him, or if he denies belief in God altogether, then he has thereby repudiated his own affirmation of God's Lordship which he as rational soul has covenanted with God. He does violence to his own Covenant, his individual contract with God. So just as in the case of one who violates his own contract brings calamity upon himself, in the same way he who does wrong or evil, who disobeys or denies God, violates the contract his soul has made with God, thereby being unjust to his soul. He has also thereby 'lied' — *kadhaba*, another apt Quranic expression — against his own self (soul). It is important in the light of this brief explanation to understand why the belief in the resurrection of bodies is fundamental in Islām, for the soul reconstituted with its former body will not be able to deny what its body had done, for its very eyes, tongue, hands and feet or limbs — the organs of ethical and moral conduct — will testify

---

81   See *al-Nisā'*(4):123; *Yūnus*(10):44

82   Analogically, the legal concept of *habeas corpus* (you must have the body) as a fundamental procedure of justice is perhaps only a mere imperfect reflection of the awesome and irrefutable Procedure to come. That the soul is capable of denial of acts of injustice is implied in *al-A'rāf* (7):172-173; and in these Verses must be seen clear evidence of the soul's capacity (*wus'*) to exercise a power (*quwwah*) of inclination

77

against its acts of injustice to itself.[82] Though in Islām injustice ostensibly applies between man and God, and between man and man, and between man and his self, in reality, however, injustice is ultimately applicable — even in the two former cases — to man's self alone; in the Islamic world view and spiritual vision, whether a man disbelieves or disobeys God, or whether he does wrong to another man, it is really to his own self that he does wrong. Injustice, being the opposite of justice, is the putting a thing in a place not its own; it is to misplace a thing; it is to misuse or to wrong; it is to exceed or fall short of the mean or limit; it is to suffer loss; it is deviation from the right course; it is disbelief of what is true, or lying about what is true knowing it to be true. Thus when a man does an act of injustice, it means that he has wronged his own soul, for he has put his soul in a place not its own; he has misused it; he has made it to exceed or fall short of its real nature; he has caused it to deviate from what is right and to repudiate the truth and to suffer loss. All that he has thus done — in one way or another — entails a violation of his Covenant with God. It is clear from what we say about injustice that justice implies *knowledge* of the right and proper place for a thing or a being to be; of right as against wrong; of the mean or limit; of spiritual gain as against loss; of truth as against falsehood. This is why knowledge (*al-ʿilm: maʿrifah: ʿilm*) occupies a most important position in Islām, where in the Holy Qur'ān alone we find more than eight hundred references to knowledge. And even in the case of knowledge, man has to do justice to it, that is, to know its limit of usefulness and not to exceed or fall short of it; to know its various orders of priority in relation to its usefulness to

---

towards right or wrong resulting in its acquisition or earning (*ḥasaba, iḥtasaba*) of good or evil. In the Islamic concept of justice and injustice outlined above, the fact that the witness to a man's actions, good or bad, is his own self is of great significance. See also *al-Nūr* (24):24.

one's self; to know where to stop and to know what can be gained and what cannot, what is true knowledge and what is learned guess and theory — in sum, to put every datum of knowledge in its right place in relation to the knowing one in such wise that what is known produces harmony in the one who knows. To know how to put what knowledge in which place is wisdom (*ḥikmah*). Otherwise, knowledge without order and seeking it without discipline does lead to confusion and hence to injustice to one's self.[83]

Knowledge, as we understand it, is of two kinds: that given by God to man; and that acquired by man by means of his own effort of rational enquiry based upon experience and observation.[84] The first kind can only be received by man through his acts of worship and devotion, his acts of service to God (*ibādāt*) which, depending upon God's grace and his own latent spiritual power and capacity created by God to receive it, the man receives by direct insight or spiritual savouring (*dhawq*) and unveiling to his spiritual vision (*kashf*). This knowledge (*ma'rifah*) pertains to his self or soul, and such knowledge — as we have touched upon cursorily in our comparison of the analogous relationship obtained between the macrocosm and the microcosm — gives insight into knowledge of God, and for that reason is the highest knowledge. Since such knowledge ultimately depends upon God's grace and because it entails deeds and works of service to God as prerequisites to its possible attainment, it follows that for it knowledge of the prerequisites becomes necessary, and this includes knowledge of the essentials of Islām (*arkān al-islām* and *arkān al-imān*), their meanings and purpose and correct

---

83 'Order' and 'discipline' here do not refer to the kind of order and discipline in the systematic deployment of knowledge found in modern universities and schools, but to the ordering of knowledge by the self that seeks to know, and to the disciplining of the self of itself to that ordering (see below pp. 83-85).

84 For further elaboration, see below, pp. 143-148.

understanding and implementation in everyday life and practice: every Muslim must have knowledge of these prerequisites, must understand the basic essentials of Islām and the Unity of God (*tawḥīd*), and practise the knowledge (*al'-ilm*) in deeds and works of service to God so that every man of Islām is in fact already in the initial stage of that first knowledge; he is set ready on the Straight Path (*ṣirāṭ al-mustaqīm*) leading to God. His further progress on the pilgrim's path depends upon his own performance and sincerity of purpose, so that some serve God as though they see Him, and others serve Him as though He sees them; and the pilgrim's progress to the former way from the latter is what constitutes the highest virtue (*iḥsān*). The second kind of knowledge (*'ilm*) is acquired through experience and observation; it is discursive and deductive and it refers to objects of pragmatical value. As an illustration of the distinction between the two kinds of knowledge we might suppose a man and his neighbour who has just moved in to his neighbourhood. At first he knows his new neighbour only by acquaintance; he might know the other's general appearance and be able to recognize him when meeting in the street; he might learn his name, his marital status, the number of his children and many other such details of information which he can obtain by observation. Then he might, through inquiries from others he knows and private investigation, discover his neighbour's occupation and place of work and appointment, and he might even find out, through further discreet investigation, how much he earns. He might go on investigating in this way without coming into direct contact with his neighbour and accumulate other data about him, and yet his knowledge of him would still be on the level of acquaintance and not of intimacy, for no matter how many more details he might add on to the knowledge about his neighbour thus acquired, there will be many more important personal details which he will never be able to know, such as the other's loves and fears and hopes and beliefs, his thoughts on life and death, his secret thoughts and feelings, his good qualities and other details such as these. Now let us suppose that he decides to know the man directly and introduces himself to him; he visits him often and eats and drinks and sports with him. Then after long years of faithful friendship and sincere companionship and devotion he might perchance receive by direct and spontaneous revelation from his friend and companion some of the many personal details and secret thoughts and feelings that are now in a flash revealed in a way which he will not be able to obtain in a lifetime of investigation and observation and research. Even this knowledge, given as a result of intimacy, is never complete, for we know that no matter how close the intimate relationship between the man and his friend — or brother, or wife and children, or parents, or lover — there will always be for him that veil of mystery that ever envelopes the one to be known like an infinite series of Chinese spherical ivory carving within carving, only to be unveiled for him by direct revelation from the other. And the other too will know by contemplating his self the infinite nature of that self that ever eludes his cognitive quest, so that even he is not able to reveal except only that which he knows. Every man is like an island set in a fathomless sea enveloped by darkness, and the loneliness his self knows is so utterly absolute because even he knows not his self completely. From this illustration we may derive certain basic conditions analogous to the first kind of knowledge. First, the desire by the one who gives knowledge about himself to be known. Second, the giving of such knowledge pertains to the same level of being, and this is because communication of ideas and feelings is possible and can be understood. Third, to be allowed to approach and know him, the one who seeks to know must abide by rules of propriety and codes of conduct and behaviour acceptable to the one who desires to be known. Fourth, his giving knowledge about himself is based on trust after a considerable period of testing of the other's sincerity and loyalty and devotion and capacity to receive — a period in which is established a firm bond of intimacy between the two. In like manner and even more so, then, is the case with knowledge given by God. In respect of the first condition, He says in the Holy Qur'ān that He has created man only that man may serve Him, and service in its profoundest sense ultimately means knowledge (*ma'rifah*), so that His purpose of creation is for the creature to know Him, as He says in a Holy Tradition (*Ḥadīth Qudsiyy*):

كنت كنزا مخفيا فاحببت ان اعرف

فخلقت الخلق لكى اعرف

"I was a Hidden Treasure, and I desired to be known, so I created Creation that I might be known."

Thus God reveals Himself to the rational soul, which possesses organs of spiritual communication and cognition such as the heart (*al-qalb*), which knows Him; the spirit (*al-rūḥ*), which loves Him; and the secret or inmost ground of the soul (*al-sirr*), which contemplates Him. Though the rational soul is not of the same level of being as God, there is yet in it that spark of Divine origin which makes it possible for it to receive communication from above and to have cognition of what is received; and from this we derive analogy for the second condition. In the case of the third condition, we say that man approaches God by sincere submission to His Will and absolute obedience to His Law; by conscious realization in himself of His Commands and Prohibitions and Ordinances, and by performance of acts of devotion and supererogatory worship approved by Him and pleasing unto Him, until such a man attains to the station in which His trust and friendship may be conferred upon him by means of knowledge given as a gift of grace to him for whom He has created the capacity to receive corresponding to the knowledge given. Thus His words in a Holy Tradition:

لا يزال عبدى يتقرب الي باالنوافل

حتى احبه فاذا احببته كنت سمعه

الذى يسمع به وبصره الذى يبصربه
ولسنه الذى ينطق به ويد ه لتي يبطش بها

"My servant ceases not to draw nigh unto Me by
supererogatory worship until I love him; and when I
love him I am his ear, so that he hears by Me, and his
eye, so that he sees by Me, and his tongue, so that he
speaks by Me, and his hand, so that he takes by Me."

As to the fourth condition of trust, it is part of the third,
and this is in itself already clear. We see then that such
knowledge, by virtue of its very nature, imparts truth and
certainty of a higher order than that obtained in knowledge
of the second kind; and because of this, and of the fact that
it pertains to the soul or self of man and its fulfilment of
the Covenant made with God, knowledge of its prerequisites, which is in fact based on this given knowledge, is
inextricably bound up with Islamic ethics and morality. By
means of such knowledge and the practice it entails we
guide and govern ourselves in daily conduct and set our
values in life and ourselves aright. The first knowledge
unveils the mystery of Being and Existence and reveals the
true relationship between man's self and his Lord, and
since for man such knowledge pertains to the ultimate
purpose for knowing, it follows that knowledge of its prerequisites becomes the basis and essential foundation for
knowledge of the second kind, for knowledge of the latter
alone, without the guiding spirit of the former, cannot truly
lead man in his life, but only confuses and confounds him
and enmeshes him in the labyrinth of endless and purposeless seeking. We also perceive that there is a limit for man
even to the first and highest knowledge; whereas no such
limit obtains in the second kind, so that the possibility of
perpetual wandering spurred on by intellectual deception
and self-delusion in constant doubt and curiosity is always
real. The individual man has no time to waste in his
momentary sojourn on earth, and the rightly guided one

knows that his individual quest for knowledge of the second kind must needs be limited to his own practical needs and suited to his nature and capacity, so that he may set both the knowledge and himself in their right places in relation to his real self and thus maintain a condition of justice. For this reason and in order to achieve justice as the end, Islām distinguishes the quest for the two kinds of knowledge, making the one for the attainment of knowledge of the prerequisites of the first obligatory to all Muslims (*farḍ 'ayn*), and that of the other obligatory to some Muslims only (*farḍ kifāyah*), and the obligation for the latter can indeed be transferred to the former category in the case of those who deem themselves duty bound to seek it for their self improvement. The division in the obligatory quest for knowledge into two categories is itself a procedure of doing justice to knowledge and to the man who seeks it, for all of the knowledge of the prerequisites of the first knowledge is good for man, whereas not all of the knowledge of the second kind is good for him, for the man who seeks that latter knowledge, which would bear considerable influence in determining his secular role and position as a citizen, might not necessarily be a *good* man. In Western civilization generally, because its conception of justice is based on secular foundations, it follows that its conception of knowledge is also based upon similar foundations, or complimentary foundations emphasizing man as a physical entity and a rational animal being, to the extent that it admits of what we have referred to as the second kind of knowledge as the only valid 'knowledge' possible. Consequently, the purpose of seeking knowledge from the lower to the higher levels is, for Western civilization, to produce in the seeker a good citizen. Islām, however, differs in this in that for it the purpose of seeking knowledge is to produce in the seeker a good man. We maintain that it is more fundamental to produce a good man than to produce a good citizen, for the good man will no doubt also be a good citizen, but the good citizen will not necessarily also be a good man. In a sense we say that Islām too maintains that the purpose of seeking knowledge is to produce in the seeker a good citizen, only that we mean by 'citizen' a Citizen of that other Kingdom, so that he acts as such even here and now as a good man. The concept of a 'good man' in Islām connotes not only that he must be 'good' in the general social sense understood, but that he must also first be good to his self, and not be unjust to it in the way we have explained, for if he were unjust to his self, how can he really be just to others? Thus we see that, already in this most fundamental concept in life — the concept of knowledge — Islām is at variance with Western civilization, in that for Islām (a) knowledge includes faith and true belief (*imān*); and that (b) the purpose for seeking knowledge is to inculcate goodness or justice in man as man and individual self, and not merely in man as citizen or integral part of society: it is man's value as a real man, as spirit, that is stressed, rather than his value as a physical entity measured in terms of the pragmatic or utilitarian sense of his usefulness to state and society and the world.

I have been describing what constitutes the very core of the Religion of Islām, and in this description have explained in brief but simple and succinct manner the fundamental concept of *dīn* and of faith and belief in Islām. I have touched upon the Islamic worldview and have stressed the paramount importance of the Quranic concept of man's Covenant with God, showing how this Covenant is of an essential nature; it is the starting point in the Islamic concept of religion, and is the dominant element in all other Islamic concepts bound up with it, such as those of freedom and responsibility, of justice, of knowledge, of virtue, of brotherhood; of the role and character of the individual and the society and of their mutual identity in the framework of the state and of collective life. I have in this description also emphasized the role of the individual, and of the individual the self, or soul, and its journey of return to God. It now behoves me to describe in outline the Islamic vision of Reality, which is no other than the philosophical core of Islām which determines its world view. Islām focusses its religious and philosophical vision (*shuhūd*) of Reality and its worldview on Being, and distinguishes between Being or Existence (*wujūd*) and its modes which are existent (*mawjūd*); between Unity (*waḥdah*) and Multiplicity (*kathrah*); between Subsistence (*baqā'*) and Evanescence (*fanā'*). This vision of Reality is based upon revealed knowledge through religious experience, and embraces both the objective, metaphysical and ontological reality as well as the subjective, mystical and psychological experience of that reality. Phenomenologically Islām, in confirmation of its vision of Reality, affirms 'being' rather than 'becoming' or 'coming-into-being', for the Object of its vision is clear, established, permanent and unchanging. This confirmation and affirmation is absolute because it springs from the certainty (*yaqīn*) of revealed knowledge; and since its Object is clear and established and permanent and unchanging, so likewise is Islām, together with its way of life and method of practice and values, an absolute reflection of the mode of the Object. Thus Islām itself is like its Object in that it emulates its ontological nature as subsisting and unchanging — as being; and hence affirms itself to be complete and perfect as confirmed by God's words in the Holy Qur'ān,[85] and it denies the possibility of ever being in need of completion or evolution towards perfection; and such concepts as *development* and *progress* and *perfection* when applied to man's life and history and destiny must indeed refer, in Islām, ultimately to the spiritual and real nature of man. If this were not so, then it can never really mean, for Islām, *true* development and progress and perfection, as it would mean only the development and progress and perfection of the animal in man; and that would not be his true evolution unless such evolution realizes in him his true nature as spirit.

Change, development and *progress,* according to the Islamic

---

85 *Al-Mā'idah* (5):4.

viewpoint, refer to the return to the genuine Islām enunciated and practised by the Holy Prophet (may God bless and give him Peace!) and his noble Companions and their Followers (blessings and peace be upon them all!) and the faith and practice of genuine Muslims after them; and they also refer to the self and mean its return to its original nature and religion (Islām). These concepts pertain to presupposed situations in which Muslims find themselves going astray and steeped in ignorance of Islām and are confused and unjust to their selves. In such situations, their endeavour to direct their selves back onto the Straight and True Path and to return to the condition of genuine Islām — such endeavour, which entails change, is development; and such return, which consists in development, is progress. Thus, for Islām, the process of movement towards genuine Islām by Muslims who have strayed away from it is development; and such development is the only one that can truly be termed as progress. Progress is neither 'becoming' or 'coming-into-being', nor movement towards that which is 'coming-into-being' and never becomes 'being', for the notion of 'something aimed at' or the 'goal' inherent in the concept 'progress' can only contain real meaning when it refers to that which is already *clear* and permanently *established*, already *being*. Hence what is already clear and established, already in the state of being, cannot suffer change, nor is it subject to constant slipping from the grasp of achievement, not constantly receding beyond attainment. The term 'progress' reflects a *definite direction* that is aligned to a *final purpose* that is meant to be achieved in life; if the direction sought is still vague, still coming-into-being, as it were, and the purpose aligned to it is not final, then how can involvement in it truly mean progress? Those who grope in the dark cannot be referred to as progressing, and they who say such people are progressing have merely uttered a lie against the true meaning and purpose of progress, and they have lied unto their selves!

مثلهم كمثل الذى استو قد نارا

فلما اضاءت ما حوله ذهب الله
بنورهم وتركهم في ظلمت لا يبصرون
صم بكم عمى فهم لا يرجعون
اوكصيب من السما فيه ظلمت
ورعد وبرق يجعلون اصا بعهم
في اذانهم من الصواعق حذ را لموت
والله محيط بالكافرين يكادا لبرق
يخطف ابصا رهم كلما اضأ لهم مشو فيه
واذا اظلم عليهم قاموولو شاء الله لذ هب بسمعهم
وابصارهم ان الله على كل شيىء قدير

Their similitude is that of a man
Who kindled a fire;
When it lighted all around him,
God took away their light
And left them in utter darkness.
So they could not see.
Deaf, dumb, and blind,
They will not return (to the path).
Or (another similitude)
Is that of a rain-laden cloud
From the sky: in it are zones
Of darkness, and thunder and lightning:
They press their fingers in their ears
To keep out the stunning thunder-clap,
The while they are in terror of death.
But God is ever round
The rejecters of Faith!
The lightning all but snatches away
Their sight; every time the light
(Helps) them, they walk therein,
And when the darkness grows on them,
They stand still.
And if God willed, He could take away
Their faculty of hearing and seeing;
For God hath power over all things.[86]

---

86 *Al-Baqarah* (2):17-20.

The Islamic worldview is not to be construed as a dualism, for although two elements are involved, yet the one is independent and subsistent while the other is dependent upon it; the one is absolute and the other relative; the one is real and the other a manifestation of that reality. So there is only One Reality and Truth, and all Islamic values pertain ultimately to It alone, so that to the Muslim, individually and collectively, all endeavour towards change and development and progress and perfection is invariably determined by the worldview that projects the vision of the One Reality and confirms the affirmation of the same Truth. In this way in practice Muslims have been able to live their lives in accordance with the belief without suffering any change to be wrought that would disrupt the harmony of Islām and of their own selves; without succumbing to the devastating touch of time, nor to the attendant challenges in the vicissitudes of worldly existence. The man of Islām has with him the Holy Qur'ān which is itself unchanged, unchanging and unchangeable; it is the Word of God revealed in complete and final form to His Chosen Messenger and Last Prophet Muḥammad (may God bless and give him Peace!). It is the clear Guidance which he carries with him everywhere, not merely literally so, but more in his tongue and mind and heart, so that it becomes the very vital force that moves his human frame. I have said earlier, when referring to man's contemplation of his self, how every man is like an island set in isolation in a fathomless sea enveloped by darkness, saying that the loneliness his self knows is so utterly absolute because even he knows not his self completely. I must add that such utter loneliness basically springs from man's inability to answer his own persistent ageless inner question to himself: "Who am I?" and "What is my ultimate destiny?" We say that such experience of utter loneliness, however, assails only the heart of the man who denies God, or doubts Him, or repudiates his soul's Covenant with God; for it is, again, recognition and affirmation of that same Covenant that established for man his identity in the order of Being and Existence. The man of Islām —

he who confirms and affirms the Covenant within his self — is never lonely for even when contemplating his self he knows intuitively, through acts of *'ibādah* that include constant recitation and reflection and contemplation of the words of God in the Holy Qur'ān, how close that self is with God, his Creator and Lord, Whom he ever contemplates in remembrance (*dhikr*) and with Whom he has intimate converse (*munājāt*). Such a man has identified his self to himself and knows his ultimate destiny, and he is secure within his self and free from the terrifying echoes of absolute loneliness and the breathless grip of silent fear. In affirmation of Being, the Holy Qur'ān, the source of Islām and projector of the Islamic worldview and the vision of the One Reality and Truth, is the expression of the finality and perfection of 'being' just as Islām is the phenomenological affirmation of 'being'; and he who conveyed the Holy Qur'ān to mankind himself represents the finality and perfection of 'being' in man. The Holy Prophet, upon whom be God's blessing and Peace!, is the Seal of the Prophets,[87] the universal and final Messenger of God to mankind,[88] whom he leads from darkness to light;[89] who is himself the Lamp spreading Light;[90] he is God's Mercy to all creatures,[91] and His favour to those who believe in him and in what he brought[92] and He is God's favour even to the People of the Book,[93] who may yet come to believe in him. He is man whom God has created with a character exalted as the standard for mankind;[94] he is the Perfect Man and Exemplar *par excellence*.[95] He it is who even God and His

---

87   *Al-Aḥzāb* (33):40.
88   *Sabā* (34):28.
89   *Al-Ṭalāq* (65):11.
90   *Al-Aḥzāb* (33):46; *al-Ṭalāq* (65):11.
91   *Al-Anbiyā'* (21):107.
92   *Ālī 'Imran* (3):164; *al-Nisā'* (4):170.
93   *Al-Mā'iduh* (5):21.
94   *Al-Qalam* (68):4.
95   *Al-Aḥzāb* (33):21.

Angels honour and bless as the greatest of men,[96] and all true Believers, in compliance with God's Command, and in emulation of His Angels, do likewise, and have done and will do so in this world and the next for as long as God wills; and in the Hereafter to him will God vouchsafe the Lauded Station.[97] Muḥammad, the Messenger of God, is he whose very name is a miracle of fulfillment for he alone among all mankind is constantly praised in every age and generation after him without end, so that even taking into account the ages and generations before him he still would be the only man to whom such praise is due. We praise him out of sincere love and respect and gratitude for having led us out of darkness into light, and he is loved above all other human beings including our selves. Our love and respect for him is such that neither time nor memory could dull, for he is in our selves in every age and generation — nay, he is closer than ourselves,[98] and we emulate his words (*qawl*) and model actions (*fi'l*) and silent confirmation (*taqrīr*) of usages known to him, so that next to the Holy Qur'ān he is our most excellent and perfect guide and exemplar in life. He is the perfect model for every Muslim male and female; adolescent, middle-aged and old, in such wise that Muslims do not suffer from the crises of identity. Because of him the external structure or pattern of Muslim society is not divided by the gap of generations such as we find prevalent in Western society. Western civilization is constantly changing and 'becoming' without ever achieving 'being', except that its 'being' is and always has been a 'becoming'. This is and has been so by virtue of the fact that it acknowledges no single, established Reality to fix its vision on; no single, valid Scripture to confirm and affirm in life; no single, human Guide whose words and deeds and actions and entire mode of life can serve as model to

---

96 *Al-Aḥzāb* (33):56.
97 *Banī Isrā'īl* (17):79.
98 *Al-Aḥzāb* (33):6.

emulate in life, but that each and every individual must find for himself and herself each one's identity and meaning of life and destiny. Western civilization affirms the evanescent (*fanā'*) aspect of reality, and its values pertain to the secular, material and physical realities of existence. Western society is thus divided by gaps between the three generations: the youth, the middle-aged, and the old. Each separate generation moves within the confines of its own attempts at finding a meaning for its own self and life in an ageless search for the answers to the questions "Who am I?" and "What is my destiny?" The youth, who at that stage experience change in life, consider the values handed down by their fathers, the middle-aged, no longer useful nor relevant to their way of life. Consequently, they do not take the middle-aged as models to guide them in life, and hence demand of them their freedom to choose *their* own destiny. The middle-aged, realizing that their values too, when they were in the prime of youth, did not succeed in guiding them in life, and now they know they are themselves unable to provide the necessary guidance for their sons, and so surrender freedom which they seek to choose their destiny in the hope that youth may yet succeed where they had failed. Now the youth, in demanding freedom to choose their own destiny, also know that they need guidance, which is unfortunately not available, for even from their very midst they are unable to bring forth a leader who can play the role of perfect model whose example can be emulated by others. This disconcerting situation creates in youth uncertainty and much doubt about the future, and they desperately dare to hope that when *they* reach the middle-age they would then be able to remould the world nearer to their heart's desire. But the middle-aged, who play the central role in moulding and preserving their state, society, and world, know from experience in their youth that their former values now no longer serve a purpose and have lost their meaning in life; and since their former search for identity has failed, so their present lives do not reflect contentment of fulfillment and are void of happiness. Thus the values they now esteem, the values that now become for them the measure of their success in searching for meaning in their individual lives, are only those promoting secular and materialistic achievements pertaining to the state and society; and so they strive and relentlessly compete among themselves to gain high places in the social ladder, or wealth and power and world renown. In the midst of such struggle, they realize that their mental capacity and intelligence are beginning to weaken; physical power and vitality are beginning to deteriorate, and consternation and regret and sadness begin to take hold of their selves when there appear in successive series before their mental perception the vision of retirement from public life into the loneliness of old age. Consequently, they look to youth with nostalgia and set high hopes that the youth may yet bring forth the longed-for perfect model and exemplar in life for all society to emulate; and this attitude towards youth is the very core of the worship of Youth, which is one of the dominant features of Western civilization since ancient times. The crisis of identity experienced by the middle-aged is somewhat similar to that experienced by the youth, with the exception that, for the middle-aged, the freedom to choose their destiny is increasingly limited, for time relentlessly moves on like a Greek tragedy to the very end. The old, in such a society, are mere creatures forgotten by society, because their very existence reminds the youth and middle-aged of what they would be like which they want to forget. The old remind them of dissolution and death; the old have lost physical power and vitality; they have lost success; they have lost memory and their use and function in society; they have lost friend and family — they have lost the future. When a society bases its philosophy of life upon secular foundations and espouses materialistic values to live by, it inevitably follows that the meaning and value and quality of life of the individual citizen therein is interpreted and measured in terms of his position as a citizen; his occupation and use and working and earning power in relation to the state. When in old age all this is gone, so likewise his identity — which is in fact moulded by the secular role he plays — is lost. The three generations that in such wise comprise Western society are forever engaged in the search for identity and meaning of life; are forever moving in the vicious circle of unattainment; each generation dissatisfied with its own self-evolved values of life; each generation finding itself a misfit. And this condition, we maintain, is what we mean by injustice (*ẓulm*). This condition is further aggravated by the fact that in Western society there exists also a crisis of identity between the sexes, in that women are engaged, as women, in the search for their own, separate identity. Islamic society is not beset by such condition. The individuals within the generations that comprise it, whether male or female, have already established their identity and recognized their ultimate destiny; the former through recognition and confirmation of the Covenant, and the latter through affirmation and realization of that Covenant by means of sincere submission to God's Will and obedience to His Law such as enacted as Islām. The man who brought to us the Holy Qur'ān as it was revealed to him by God, who thus brought to us the Knowledge of our identity and destiny, whose own life is the most excellent and perfect interpretation of the Holy Qur'ān so that his life becomes for us the focus of emulation and true guiding spirit, is the Holy Prophet, may God bless and give him Peace! By his teaching and example he has shown us the right and true practice of Islām and of Islamic virtues; he is the perfect model not merely for one generation, but for all generations; not merely for a time, but for all time. Indeed, we say that the concept 'perfect model' can fulfill its true meaning only if he who is thus described, such as Muḥammad alone is, embodies within his self all the permanent human and spiritual values necessary for man's guidance in life, whose validity is such that they serve man not only for the span of his individual lifetime, but for as long as man lives in this world. So every generation of Muslims, emulating his example, passes on the way of life he patterned to the next in such wise that no gaps nor crises of identity occur between them, but that each preceding generation guides the next by confirming and affirming his example in their lives.

IV

THE MUSLIM DILEMMA

The major problems that beset Muslim society today must be understood against the background of historical confrontation which Western culture and civilization had perpetuated against Islām, and whose causes are to be traced from the earliest periods in the formation of Christianity before the advent of Islām. One of the definitions of knowledge is to know the cause of the existence of a thing, for knowledge of the cause leads to knowledge of the nature of the thing caused. Thus knowledge of the cause, or causes, of the dilemma in which we find ourselves today is itself a partial solution to the problem. For this reason it is important for us to discern the underlying causes that pose critical problems for us today, of which some have their origins within our own world and our own intellectual history, and some originated from without as effects of the confrontation alluded to above. From the point of view of their critical impact upon our lives it matters little whether these problems originated from within or without, as they all create equally destructive consequences for our society and Community. It is important to know whether there is such a confrontation, and if so to know why and how it happened and what its nature is that it should persist in history and in the present and future.

That Western culture and civilization, which includes Christianity as an integral part of it, has been assuming the posture of confrontation against Islām there can be no doubt. The root cause of the confrontation is to be discerned in the origins of Christianity and the rise of Islām as

I understand them and as I will attempt to convey in the cursory sketch that now follows.

We must visualize the religious situation in the world centuries before the advent of Islām when Christianity was in the process of formation. It would not have been the least difficult for the early religious authorities among the Christians — the thinkers and theorists — to realize when they assessed their position in the world that of all the great world religions known at the time Christianity alone possessed not only the potentiality and capacity to become, like the others, a world religion, but more important to be developed into a *universal* religion that would dominate over nations and world affairs. They would have clearly seen, gazing with their mind's eye upon the vista of world religions known at the time, that neither Judaism, nor Zoroastrianism, nor Hinduism and Buddhism, nor Confucianism could in fact develop into a world force as a universal religion. Indeed at that time these religions had already existed many centuries before the new religion, and none of them went beyond the confines of their own nations and cultures and worlds, but remained as if insulated within their own domains and spheres of influence in the peripheral regions that surrounded them. This was truly so by virtue of the fact that in the case of Judaism it was a national religion restricted only to a small and persecuted race occupying the lands of the diaspora; and as such it could not and did in fact not disseminate itself to other nations of the world. Zoroastrianism too was national in character, though not in essence as in the case of Judaism, in that it was peculiar to the cultural and traditional traits of the ancient Persians which could not possibly be adopted by other nations of the world. The same was true in the case of Hinduism and Buddhism, which did not possess doctrines of salvation like the one Christianity was formulating, and hence they did not possess the salvific spirit of *mission* which was necessary to make religion universally acknowledged. This was no doubt a great factor that accounted for the fact of their insulation within their own regions in spite of their long preexistence comparable with the others. No doubt Buddhism did spread to China and Japan and Southeast Asia, as also did Hinduism in the region last mentioned, but this was not necessarily because of any salvific spirit of mission; and moreover their influence extended only among the peoples of the peripheral regions. Confucianism, like Judaism, was likewise a national religion. In this case the worship of ancestors made it impossible for peoples other than Chinese to become Confucians, and Confucianism was thus meant only for the Chinese so that it too could not possibly be adopted by the various nations of the world. Furthermore it was not a religion in the sense understood particularly by the adherents of 'revealed' religions. Thus in this brief summing up of the religious situation in the world before the advent of Islām, and the assessment of the future role of Christianity, the astute minds and self-conscious perception of the pioneers of the new religion must indeed have realized the tremendous role open to Christianity in that it alone could develop into a universal religion.

Now the very idea of universality in religion is itself unique and revolutionary in its effect upon human life, for no cosmopolitan life, no universal citizenship, is possible and conceivable unless the God of religion is also a Universal God. In his book *The Ancient City*,[99] Numa Denis Fustel de Coulanges, a French thinker and historian of ideas, says that the Greek *polis* never became universal because what was missing was the Universal God of Christianity.[100] According to him Christianity preached a universal religion from its first appearance, for it called to the whole human race.[101] In reality however, and according to our view, the *idea* of universality in religion, in spite of the claim of theologians and other Western thinkers that it was Christianity that originated it, and that only after the

---

99 New York, 1956; see Book III, chapters 3–5.
100 *Ibid.*, p. 151.
101 *Ibid.*, p. 391.

beginning of Christianity were its implications regarding universal citizenship possible to realize, was not originally Christian. According to the Holy Qur'ān the true religion was from the very beginning universal since it refers to one and the same Universal God. It was thus God Who revealed to man the universal religion. But man gradually forgot and aberrations in religion became common among men so that from time to time God had to reveal the universal religion again and again through His Prophets and Messengers. The idea of the universal religion did not originate in man's intellect and gradually evolve and develop in his culture and history. It was revealed to him by God, otherwise he would not be able to conceive it. This was why in spite of the great intellectual achievements of Greek and other sages and philosophers of antiquity reflecting the brilliance and originality of their ideas, they never conceived a universal religion. Since we have earlier stated that Christianity is not, strictly speaking, a revealed religion, but that it is a culture religion created by man and that it evolved and developed in history,[102] whence then and how did the idea of a universal religion come to be claimed as having originated in Christianity? The answer according to what can be interpreted from the Holy Qur'ān is that God revealed to Jesus (on whom be Peace!) the coming of the Holy Prophet (may God bless and give him Peace!) who would finally establish among mankind the Universal Religion (Islām). Jesus (on whom be Peace!) informed his disciples about what God had revealed to him and preached concerning it to his followers. But those who later altered the substance of his teachings, appropriated this idea of a universal religion and applied it to their own new creation. So the so-called Christian idea of a universal religion was taken from the sermons of Jesus (on whom be Peace!) *where he meant it to refer to Islām,* but which was later appropriated for the new religion Christianity. God's Plan, however, can neither be confounded nor prevented from

---

102 See above, pp. 20–25; 27–29.

coming to pass, for in spite of its first claim to what in fact was borrowed and artificially created universality, and a head start of six centuries preceding Islām, Christianity naturally never fully realized it in history. The realization in history of the true universal religion still became a fact with the advent of Islām, when from the very beginning of its manifestation it addressed itself to the whole of mankind and forged a firm bond of brotherhood among members of its multiracial Community, the like of which was never seen nor would ever be seen in any other religion. Within less than a century after its advent, the Community of Islām comprised not only of Arabs and other Semites, but also Persians, Egyptians, Berbers, Europeans, Africans, Indians, Chinese, Turks, and Malays. Islām did not have to wait for almost two millenia to realize its universal character.

The rise of Islām changed the world; and in the wake of global changes great and far reaching repercussions occurred in the West and within Christianity itself. The rapid dissemination of Islām throughout the world caused two major historic events in the West which shaped its subsequent history and destiny. One was the dissolution of the cultural unity of the Mediterranean basin, which had for centuries moulded the way of life of the peoples of the surrounding regions; the other was the consequent shift in the axis of Western Christian life from Rome to the North centered around Aix Ia Chapelle where the new Carolingian dynasty had assumed power and temporal leadership of Western civilization. These two major events not only changed Western culture and civilization in 'body', but in 'spirit' as well; and these two significant events in the history of a civilization were rightly considered by the Belgian historian, Henri Pirenne, as the true historical criteria which supported his thesis that it was the rise and expansion of Islām that brought about the beginnings of the Middle Ages in Western history.[103] Christianity itself suffered a separation

---

103 See his two important works: *A History of Europe*, London, 1967; and *Muhammad and Charlemagne*, London, 1958.

101

of destinies between Rome and Constantinople; the one moulding itself more and more into the forms of the Western European cultural traditions and the other assuming its Byzantine identity. Apart from the influences which went deep into the religion of the West, Islām also caused revolutionary changes in the linguistic, social, cultural, political and economic aspects of Western life. Muslim centers of learning in the West radiated knowledge to the Western world, and with that knowledge Western scholars, thinkers and theologians were able to regain their lost intellectual legacies òf ancient civilizations, which later were to exert such great influence in nurturing the spirit of their Renaissance. Although Scholasticism had its roots in the earlier patristical period, the rise of Islām and its expansion in the West, which caused the Carolingian renaissance in the 9th century, may be regarded as the beginning of its history of significant development up till the 12th century. Between the 9th and the 13th centuries Muslim philosophers like al-Kindī, al-Fārābī, ibn Sīnā and ibn Rushd — particularly the latter two — had been instrumental in shaping the intellectual preparation of Scholasticism as the philosophy of Christian society towards attainment to its Golden Age in the 13th century with the official adoption of Aristotelianism into Christian theology and metaphysics.[104] Ibn Sinā's method influenced men like Albert the Great, the teacher of Thomas Aquinas, and Henri of Ghent and the many disciples of Bonaventure of Bagnoregio including Duns Scotus and Meister Eckhart. His conceptual distinction between essence and existence, in which existence is conceived on the one hand as accident to essence, and on the other as the very substance of it, have influence Aquinas himself in his own distinction between essence and existence which effected a revolutionary change in Christian theology and metaphysics and whose effect and implications dominated Christian

---

104 See above, pp. 8–11; 33–38.

philosophy and theology up to this day.[105] Aquinas was also indebted to ibn Sīnā on the idea that the universal had real existence only as creative idea in God; that it had experiential existence only in individual things; and that it had mental existence when abstracted from the particulars of the human mind. These were ideas that, in the mind of a genius like Aquinas, played an important role in the formulation of Christian theology and metaphysics and contributed to the emergence of the Golden Age of Scholasticism. Apart from Muslim philosophers, Ṣūfīs—such as ibn 'Arabī, to mention one great example—also played significant roles in the development of Christian mysticism represented by men like Dante Alighieri and Raymond Lull in the 14th century.

From the very beginning of its advent Islām challenged Christianity's right to universality. Then in its earliest Revelations received at Makkah it challenged the authenticity and truth of fundamental Christian doctrines.[106] Then Islām followed up these tremendous doctrinal challenges, which amounted to the challenge to valid existence and hence also to world domination, by historically unprecedented rapid territorial expansion whose extent stretched far and wide—greater than any known empire the world had seen. Together with these extraordinary events, which in themselves caused traumatic and harrowing experiences in Western Christian life and spirit, Islām carried to the West superior knowledge and the spirit of intellectual and rational investigation of higher truths that was to set the pace in the development of Western Christian intellectual history. Finally, it was because of Islām's supremacy in world affairs and the economic blockade effected by Islām upon the West beginning from the 9th to the 14th centuries in its control of world trade and trade routes—both

---

105 See above, pp. 8–11.
106 See e.g., *al-Ikhlāṣ.* (122); see also the references in note 30, above.

the land and sea routes—that forced the West to live in isolation and on its own means and efforts, and to seek other ways to the sources of international supplies. In that quest, which was prompted by the direct involvement of Islām in world history and in Western intellectual history, the West was able, after the Reconquista in the 15th and 16th centuries, to gather its strength and intellectual resources; to emerge once again on the stage of world history as a dynamic force achieving many far reaching 'discoveries' for itself such as — apart from scientific 'discoveries' — the 'discovery' of America by Amerigo Vespucci and Christopher Columbus; the 'discovery' of the sea route to India *via* the Cape of Good Hope by Vasco da Gama with the assistance of his Muslim pilot who already knew the way; and thence to the Spice Islands of the Malay Archipelago, and its first adventure in colonization with the capture of the strategic seaports and stapling points in the Indian Ocean, and in the Straits of Malacca by Alfonso d'Albuquerque.

What is briefly sketched above is meant to underline the fact that Islām played the dominant role in the *shaping of world history* from the time of its advent onwards at least for a thousand years. The Western counter-attack came gradually beginning with the scientific revolution in Western-Europe in the 13th century and its gradual growth in subsequent centuries in military and economic power. The geographical expansion of Western Europe eastwards and westwards and the establishment of its trading posts in the Indian Ocean in the 16th century caused grave economic repercussions in the Muslim world. The progressive weakening of the Muslim world, which was primarily caused by internal elements whose germs were evident in the early periods of Islām, had made possible the Western colonization of a significant part of that world from the 17th century onwards till own times; and with the colonization and cultural control of vital areas of the Muslim world, the West was able to inculcate the projection of its worldview in the Muslim mind and thence to dominate the Muslims intellectually. The dissemination of the basic essentials of the Western worldview and its surreptitious consolidation in the Muslim mind was gradually accomplished through the educational system based upon a concept of knowledge and its principles that would ultimately bring about the deislamization of the Muslim mind. The confrontation between Western culture and civilization and Islām, from the historical and religious and military levels, has now moved on to the intellectual level; and we must realize, then, that this confrontation is by nature a historically *permanent* one. Islām is seen by the West as posing a challenge to its very way of life; a challenge not only to Western Christianity, but also to Aristotelianism and the epistemological and philosophical principles deriving from Graeco-Roman thought which forms the dominant component integrating the key elements in the dimensions of the Western worldview. The West is ever bound to regard Islām as the true rival in the world; as the only abiding force confronting it and challenging its basic beliefs and principles. And the West and Islām as well know that the dispute between them revolves around fundamental issues to which no compromise is possible. In the perpetual clash of worldviews between Islām and the West is to be discerned the external sources and causes, *in esse* and *in posse*, of the problems that beset us today.

As to the internal causes of the dilemma in which we find ourselves, the basic problems can — it seems to me — be reduced to a single evident crisis which I would simply call the *loss of adab*. I am here referring to the loss of *discipline* — the discipline of body, mind, and soul; the discipline that assures the recognition and acknowledgement of one's proper place in relation to one's self, society and Community; the recognition and acknowledgement of one's proper place in relation to one's physical, intellectual, and spiritual capacities and potentials; the recognition and acknowledgement of the fact that knowledge and being are ordered hierarchically. Since *adab* refers to *recognition* and *acknowledgement* of the right and proper place, station, and condition in life and to self discipline in positive and willing participation in enacting one's role in accordance with that recognition and acknowledgement, its occurrence in one and in society as a whole reflects the condition of justice. Loss of *adab* implies loss of justice, which in turn betrays confusion in knowledge. In respect of the society and community, the confusion in knowledge of Islām and the Islamic worldview creates the condition which enables false leaders to emerge and to thrive, causing the condition of injustice. They perpetuate this condition since it ensures the continued emergence of *leaders* like them to replace them after they are gone, perpetuating their domination over the affairs of the Community. Thus to put it briefly in their proper order, our present general dilemma is caused by:

1. Confusion and error in knowledge, creating the condition for:
2. The loss of *adab* within the Community. The condition arising out of (1) and (2) is:
3. The rise of leaders who are not qualified for valid leadership of the Muslim Community, who do not possess the high moral, intellectual and spiritual standards required for Islamic leadership, who perpetuate the condition in (1) above and ensure the continued control of the affairs of the Community by leaders like them who dominate in all fields.

All the above roots of our general dilemma are interdependent and operate in a vicious circle. But the chief cause is confusion and error in knowledge, and in order to break this vicious circle and remedy this grave problem, we must first come to grips with the problem of loss of *adab*, since no true knowledge can be instilled without the precondition of *adab* in the one who seeks it and to whom it is imparted. Thus, for sublime example, God Himself commands that the Holy Qur'ān, the Fountain of all true knowledge, cannot even be touched in approach save through the prescribed *adab* of ritual purity. Indeed, *'ibādah* in its entirety is but another expression of *adab* towards God. Knowledge must be approached reverently and in humility, and it cannot be possessed simply as if it were there available to everyone irrespective of intention and purpose and capacity. Where knowledge of Islām and the Islamic world view is concerned, it is based on authority. Since Islām is already established in perfection from the very beginning, requiring no further developmental change nor evolution towards perfection, we say again that adequate knowledge about Islām is always possible for all Muslims. There can be no relativism in the historical interpretation of Islām, so that knowledge about it is either right or wrong, or true or false, where wrong and false means contradiction with the already established and clear truth, and right and true means conformity with it. Confusion about such truth means simply ignorance of it, and this is due not to any inherent vagueness or ambiguity on the part of that truth. The interpretation and clarification of knowledge about Islām and the Islamic world view is accomplished by authority, and legitimate authority recognizes and acknowledges a hierarchy of authorities culminating in the Holy Prophet, upon whom be Peace! It is incumbent upon us to have a proper attitude towards legitimate authority, and that is reverence, love, respect, humility and intelligent trust in the veracity of the knowledge interpreted and clarified by such authority. Reverence, love, respect, humility and intelligent trust can only be realized in one when one recognizes and acknowledges the fact that there is a hierarchy in the human order and in authority within that hierarchy in point of *intelligence, spiritual knowledge* and *virtue.* In respect of the human order in society, we do not in the least mean by 'hierarchy' that semblance of it wherein oppression and exploitation and domination are legitimized as if they were an established principle ordained by God. *Any* kind of "hierarchy" or "order" is not necessarily legitimate, for such order is not order at all — it is *disorder,* and *adab* is not resignation to disorder as that would be contrary to justice. Disorder is the manifestation of the occurrence of injustice. The fact that hierarchical disorders have prevailed in human society does not mean that hierarchy in the human order is not valid, for there is, in point of fact, *legitimate* hierarchy in the order of creation, and this is the Divine Order pervading all Creation and manifesting the occurrence of justice. God is the Just, and He fashions and deploys all Creation in justice. In order that mankind generally might recognize and acknowledge the just order, He has bestowed upon His Prophets, Messengers and men of piety and spiritual discernment the wisdom and knowledge of it so that they in turn might convey it to mankind who ought to conform with it as individual and as society. And this conformity with that order is the occurrence of *adab*; the resulting condition of that conformity is justice. Human society is not necessarily by nature made up of equal elements. From the mineral to the vegetal to the animal kingdoms of nature we discern orders of hierarchy from the lowest to the highest. Even among angels there are those in the highest level nearest to God (*al-muqarrabūn*). And in the Hereafter too Heaven and Hell and their respective inhabitants would all be likewise ordered from the highest to the lowest. In respect of the individual, the confusion in knowledge of Islām and the Islamic worldview very often creates in him an overweening sort of individualism: he thinks himself the equal of others who are in reality superior to him, and cultivates immanent arrogance and obstinacy and tends to reject authority. He thinks he knows whereas in reality he does not know his place in relation to himself and to others; and he inclines towards envy. In that condition he allows his passions to hold sway over his actions and decisions in life. While God declares that He does not burden a soul more than what it can bear[107] — which reveals that even souls are not equal in capacity — the individual we mean, instigated by his own arrogant ambitions and disposition, does not hesitate to wrongly burden his soul by

---

107 See *al-Baqarah* (2): 286.

taking upon himself a trust and responsibility — whether political, social, cultural, intellectual, religious and spiritual — which he in his real capacity cannot adequately fulfill. When people like him increase in number some of them, or those they consider representative of their kind, inevitably become leaders who we have earlier designated as false. And they consolidate their kind in all spheres of responsibility and trust in societal life: the political, social, cultural, intellectual, religious and spiritual. The resulting condition suffered by the society is what we have called the loss of *adab*, which reflects the injustice that prevails, and the continued corruption of knowledge.

Now it may be that many Muslims today, when reminded of the preponderantly false character of those to whom they have entrusted the responsibility to lead them, ask how we are to know their rightful places; to be able to distinguish the true from the false; to ensure that the true will be in their rightful places and the false in theirs, and hence to ensure deliverance from the tyranny and misguidance of false leaders? Indeed, this very question in fact demonstrates clearly the rampant confusion that has already taken hold of our minds. Only when Muslims are immersed in ignorance can such a question be raised, for the mere fact that God has commanded that we render back our trusts (*an tu'addū 'l-amānāt*) to those to whom they are due (*ilā ahlihā*) means that *we ought already to know* the true from the false and the right from the wrong in the matter of entrusting the responsibility of right leadership — otherwise He would not have so commanded. The fact that we now raise the question means that we have lost that capacity for discernment necessary to distinguish the true from the false and the right from the wrong, and in such a state we must realize that the *answer* to it *will not be understood* unless we regain that knowledge which is *adab*. We must not forget that Islām is not a religion meant for fools, and this means that we must constantly refresh our knowledge of Islām and the Islamic worldview and be vigilant against false interpretations; that we must always rise to the level of that correct knowledge of Islām and the Islamic worldview so that whatever else of knowledge of the sciences that we might seek will always be set in proper balance with the former in such wise as to maintain a just order of knowledge in ourselves. The manner as to how this condition can be accomplished will be clarified in the next chapter, where a possible solution to the problem is outlined in the form of a systematic organization of a plan of education that reflects Islām and its worldview.

Now we have said earlier that the progressive weakening of the Muslim world was primarily caused by internal elements whose germs were discernible in the early periods of Islām; and we said further, with reference to these internal elements, that they created the condition of loss of *adab*. The chief characteristic symptom of loss of *adab* within the Community is the process of levelling that is cultivated from time to time in the Muslim mind and practiced in his society. By 'levelling' I mean the *levelling* of everyone, in the mind and the attitude, to the same level of the leveller. This mental and attitudinal process, which impinges upon action, is perpetrated through the encouragement of false leaders who wish to demolish legitimate authority and valid hierarchy so that they and their like might thrive, and who demonstrate by example by levelling the great to the level of the less great, and then to that of the still lesser. This Jāhilī streak of individualism, of immanent arrogance and obstinacy and the tendency to challenge and belittle legitimate authority, seems to have perpetrated itself — albeit only among extremists of many sorts — in all periods of Muslim history. When Muslims become confused in their knowledge of Islām and its world view, these extremists tend to spread among them and influence their thinking and infiltrate into positions of religious leadership, then their leadership in all spheres of life tends to exhibit this dangerous streak and to encourage its practice among Muslims as if it were in conformity with the teachings of Islām. They who encourage this attitude pretend that what is encouraged is no other than the egalitarian principle of Islām, whereas in fact it is far from it in that what they propagate leads to the destruction, or at least the undermining of legitimate authority and hierarchy in the human order — it is the levelling of all to *their level*; it is injustice. Some earlier Muslims who exhibited this streak of levelling, of whittling down to *their* size their great contemporaries or predecessors, have invariably concentrated their censure on the fact that those great and true leaders of the Community were mere human beings, men of flesh and blood like any other, and have emphasized their human errors which were in reality trivial in nature in comparison with their individual learning and wisdom and virtue and considerable contributions to the knowledge of Islām and its worldview. Moreover, these so-called errors and mistakes do not in the least negate the validity of their thoughts reflected in their works and their deeds, nor of their rightful places in the life of the Community throughout the ages. Indeed, even the Noble Companions — may God be well pleased with them — were not exempt from such censure: Sayyidinā 'Umar and Sayyidinā 'Alī were both charged by a lesser man with committing mistakes, notwithstanding the fact that, according to a well-known *hadīth*, they were both included among the Ten who were assured Paradise. We can only marvel how, when God Himself has overlooked their mistakes, a mere creature who lived centuries later could still persist in pointing out those mistakes! No doubt it is possible to concede that the critics of the great and learned were in the past at least themselves great and learned in their own way, but it is a mistake to put them together on the same level — the more so to place the lesser above the greater in rank as it happens in the estimation of our age of greater confusion. In our own times those who know cannot fail to notice that critics of the great and learned and virtuous among Muslims, who emulate the example of their teachers in the habit of censuring their own true leaders, are men invariably much less in authoritative worth than the lesser of the past; men whose intellectual and spiritual

111

perception of Islām and its world view cannot even be compared with any of those of their teachers — let alone with those of the great they disparage, from whom their teachers did derive knowledge and guidance without due acknowledgement. Not a single one of the so-called Modernists and Reformers of our times, including those who masquerade as *'ulamā'* barely reaches the lowest level of the great *'ulamā'* of the past and men of spiritual discernment who contributed so much to the knowledge of Islām and the Islamic world view, whether in terms of intelligence, virtue and spiritual knowledge, or in terms of volume in original, individual analyses, interpretations, commentaries and other written efforts. In fact, they never produced such works, their writings being largely of a journalistic nature and content. In the beginning, they had to air their views about such questions as the createdness or uncreatedness of the Holy Qur'ān, and many dabbled in the vexed question of *qaḍā* and *qadr* — they had to imitate the great of the past in order to gain the confidence and credulity of the confused. And those who judge them as great leaders are those who do not truly know the real ones of the past. For all the questions and problems that they attempted to raise and solve had already been dealt with with keener and profounder insight and with more intellectual and spiritual sophistication and refinement by men like al-Ash'arī, al-Ghazālī, the Ahl al-Taṣawwuf and other masters of the past. Moreover, the nature of the Holy Qur'ān and of *qaḍā* and *qadr* and related questions are not considered as problems by Muslims who *know* and *believe*, and their being presented as if they are problems only betrays their confusion and adds to the general confusion that has invaded our minds and our belief and faith. Such exercises serve only to advocate the affectation of those who set themselves up as equals of their masters. They and their followers thrive where there is confusion and ignorance, where they can escape the relentless scrutiny and censure of knowledge. It is because Muslims in our age have become confused and ignorant and desperate that they see men who have, as if for the first time, opened their minds to Islām; they do not see that these men are poor imitations of the great of the past. They do not bring anything new that the illustrious Muslims of the past have not already brought; nor do they clarify Islām better to the clouded vision than the immensely superior clarification accomplished by the masters of the past. Yet, it is such as they who have been most vociferous and vehement in disparaging and denouncing the past and its great the learned scholars and thinkers and jurists and men of spiritual discernment. Their conception of the past has been influenced by Western ideas on human evolution and historical development and secular science. These ideas are the second serious instance — the first being those of the Falāsifah whom al-Ghazālī vanquished—of the smuggling of Western concepts alien to Islām into the Muslim mind. But the Falāsifah at least understood Western thought better than they, and although these Modernists and Reformers were cautious in attempting to islamize the ideas they brought in, their ideas pose a great danger to the Muslim's loyalty to Islām because they were not ideas that could be truly islamized. They opened the doors to secularism without knowing it, for it did not take long for their followers to develop their ideas to secular proportions. The great Muslims of the past were not really their intellectual ideals; people like Rousseau, Comte, Mill, and Spencer were more properly their intellectual ideals. Islām in reality did not seem to be the principle of their thought; they attempted to fit Islām to their ideals. Though they claim to be Muslims, their loyalty is to their country, which loyalty seems to be levelled to the same plane as that due to Islām. Because they were never really intellectually and spiritually profound, they preoccupied themselves instead with sociology and politics. Their experience of the decline of Muslim rule and the disintegration of Muslim empires made them take notice of Ibn Khaldūn and they concentrated their efforts on the concept of *ummah* and of the state in Islām. They naturally neglect to lay as much stress on the concept of the individual and the role the individual plays in realizing and establishing the *ummah* and the Islamic state. Now it is true that the *ummah* and the Islamic state are paramount in Islām, but so is the individual Muslim, for how can the *ummah* and the Islamic state be developed and established if individually Muslims have become confused and ignorant about Islām and its world view and are no longer *good* Muslims? When they say that the decline of the Muslims was caused by corrupt leadership, their identification of cause with *corrupt leadership* is not quite correct. If we ask ourselves what is it that is corrupt about their leadership we will recognize at once that it is their *knowledge* that is corrupt which renders their leadership corrupt. Corrupt leadership is the effect, and not the cause; and it is the *effect* of confusion and error in knowledge of Islām and its worldview. If we accept this, then it ought to be clear that the root of the problem is no longer to be seen as grounded in the *ummah* and the state. The identification of cause with the corruption of *knowledge* as here suggested, and not with that of *leadership* as they suggest, significantly shifts the ground wherein lies the root of the problem to that of knowledge, and knowledge is inherent in *man* as *individual,* and not in society and state and *ummah.* So, *as a matter of correct strategy* in our times and under the present circumstances, it is important to stress the individual in seeking a just solution to our problem rather than the society and the state. Stressing the individual implies, as a precondition for our ideas to be equipped sufficiently to enable us to grasp and present a solution to the problem, knowledge about the intelligence, virtue, and the spirit, and about ultimate destiny and purpose; for intelligence, virtue, and the spirit are elements inherent in the individual, and such knowledge is to be gained not from Western notions of psychology, which are irrelevant to us, but from Islamic tradition expounded and interpreted by our masters of the past, the men of spiritual discernment. Only in this way can we conceptualize and then realize an educational system within the Quranic framework and based upon Islamic foundations that would educate generations of Muslims to come to become *good* Muslims; Muslims no longer confused, but knowing and practicing and ready to realize and establish the Islamic state and to enact their proper role as a single, vigorous *ummah*. Otherwise — if the preoccupation is only with the *ummah* and the state—efforts to realize our purpose will be doomed to failure such as we have experienced; and our enemies and the ignorant intent upon confounding us will say, as they have said and are saying, that Islām is no longer 'relevant' today, and that the Islamic state is merely an ideal that cannot be established and practised in fact. The stressing of society and the state opens the door to secularism and secular ideology and secular education. Now, we already possess an abundant store of knowledge about the intelligence, virtue and the spirit, and of teachers in the masters of the past who were men possessed of intellectual and spiritual discernment and virtue; all these — the knowledge and the men — of a universal quality and character, so that what they brought forth is valid for man for all time, since the Sources whence such knowledge comes, and the deep draughts such men drew, are of a universal nature so unique in its transcending of history and the forces of change that they are always new, always 'modern'. If the modernist 'reformers' really knew, they would at least have benefitted from them. But such knowledge and such men were precisely the ones they ignored, in spite of the fact that the Sources referred to are the Holy Qur'ān and the Sunnah. Instead, they disparaged such men and looked for faults and condemned the men because of their faults, notwithstanding their merits being greater than their faults. *Adab* consists in the discernment of the merits, not of the faults; for the merits determine their place in the hierarchical order.

There is not much fundamental difference in basic ideas and in issues formulated and in character and quality between the modernist 'reformers' and their counterpart the traditionalist 'reformers' of our times, for they all derive their example from the same line of critics among the *'ulamā'* of less authoritative worth who in earlier times preoccupied themselves with denigrating their greater contemporaries and predecessors. All are prone to levelling everyone to the same level of equality, notwithstanding the fact that even in God's Sight we are not all the same and equal. Indeed, we are all the same in point of being creatures of God, in point of being human beings, cast in flesh and blood. But our spirits, our souls, though derived from that One Spirit, and though *essentially* the same are, in point of *power* and *magnitude,* not the same, not equal. We are like so many candles of varying lengths and shapes and hues and sizes; the tallow they are made from is essentially the same and the light they burn is essentially the same, but the greatness of the flame, the light each sheds is not the same in power and magnitude. And we judge the value of the candle by the light it sheds just as we judge a man by those qualities by which he is not the *same,* but *excels* another such as by intelligence, virtue, and spiritual discernment. So it is neither correct nor true to regard such a man as merely a man of flesh and blood *like any other,* for he is not like any other in that his intelligence, virtue, and spiritual discernment transcend the limitations of his flesh and blood, and his greatness of spirit manifests his excellence over others. *Adab* is the recognition and acknowledgement of such lights in man; and acknowledgement entails an attitude expressing true reverence, love, respect, humility — it entails knowing one's proper place in relation to him who sheds such light. But these traditionalist 'reformers', in spite of the fact that they are men of far lesser lights than the luminaries of the past, whose lights in fact vanish when set against *their* brilliance, who all too willingly play at 'reforming' to a confused audience unable to assess truly the quality of the 'reform' other than by its own inadequate criteria of estimation, all too frequently become puffed up with their own self-importance. They are like a signpost on the Way to the Truth that instead of pointing the traveller along the Way to other earlier, clearer signposts nearer the Truth, point to itself and so confuse. They and their followers, who have become insensibly more arrogant than the leaders, have done something which no group or school in earlier times ever contemplated doing; and that is to popularize the idea that the Holy Prophet, upon whom be Peace, is no more than a man like any other man. They do this by constantly underlining the *āyat* in the Holy Qur'ān where God, Glorious and Exalted, commands the Holy Prophet, Peace be upon him, to say that he is 'but a man like you all'.[108] Their underlining of the *āyat* and incessant quoting of it is to remind us of the fact that Muḥammad, who may God bless and give Peace, is not an angel or a god or God incarnate, but a man and a mortal. Why should they do this? — have we all become unbelievers that they should direct us to reflect upon that fact? They must know that the *āyat* they glibly quote as if discovered for the first time is meant actually *to be directed towards unbelievers.* Other *āyāt* occur in the Holy Qur'ān where the other Prophets, upon whom be Peace, are also commanded to say the same thing, and all of them are directed towards unbelievers.[109] Believers *already know* that Prophets are men, and *already believe* in them and in what they brought, so that there is no need to tell believers that Prophets all are men. Indeed, that is why believers *believe.* They must see that to believers God, Glorious and Most Exalted, tells them that the Holy Prophet, upon whom be Peace, is the Seal of the Prophets; the Universal and Final Messenger of god to mankind; the Lamp spreading Light; God's Mercy to all creatures; exalted in character and nature as the standard for mankind; the Examplar *par excellence* — and many more.[110] God

---

108 *Al-Kahf* (18): 110.

109 See for example, *al-An'ām* (6): 91; *Ibrāhīm* (14): 10–11; *Banī Isrā'īl*(17): 93–94; *al-Kahf* (18): 110; *al-Anbiyā'* (21): 3; *al-Mu'minūn* (23): 24, 33: *al-Shu'arā'* (26): 153 *Yā Sīn* (36): 15; *Ḥā Mīm* (41): 6; *Al-Qamar* (54): 24; *al-Taghābūn* (64): 6.

110 See the references in notes 87–98 above.

has established in our hearts recognition and acknowledgement of his superiority and excellence over all other
men; and it is these supreme qualities of the Holy Prophet,
upon whom be Peace, that must be stressed to the Muslim
audience of all ages. They may say that in our age of aberrations and excesses in belief and faith, an age in which
they think that Muslims are on the verge of unbelief, it is
proper and timely to emphasize the human and mortal
nature of the Holy Prophet, upon whom be Peace. We
answer that even if what they allege and think is true, and
even if there is genuine good intention in what they do,
they still fail to see that the general confusion of the
Muslims has not been and is not caused by any confusion
on the part of the Muslims as to the nature and personality
and mission of the Holy Prophet, upon whom be Peace.
Confusion in belief and faith among the Muslims has nothing to do with and does not revolve around any issue
relating to the Holy Prophet's humanity and created
nature. The cause lies not in confusion about the created
nature of the Holy Prophet, but in ignorance of *tawḥīd* and
the fundamental articles of faith and other related
essentials of belief which are all comprised in that category
of knowledge which we have designated as *farḍu'ayn*; and
this means that the cause is part of the general cause which
we have in this chapter called confusion and error in knowledge. The basic problem, therefore, is that of education—
the lack of proper and adequate Islamic *education* — for
such education, rightly systematized, would assuredly pre-
vent the occurrence of general confusion leading to aberrations and excesses in belief and in practice. The rise of
false leaders in all spheres of life which follows from loss of
adab and confusion and error in knowledge respectively
means in this particular case the rise of false *'ulamā'* who
restrict knowledge (*al-'ilm*) to the domain of jurisprudence
(*fiqh*). They are not worthy followers of the *mujtahidūn*; the
great Imāms who through their individual efforts of
sublime research established the Schools of Law and Jurisprudence in Islām. They are not men of keen intelligence

and profound insight, nor are they men of integrity in keeping the trust of right spiritual leadership. Notwithstanding the fact that the Holy Qur'ān repeatedly condemns it, they delight in endless controversy, disputations and polemics which succeed only in making mountains out of jurisprudential molehills in whose blind paths the generality of Muslims are left guideless and bewildered. Their misguidance leads to the emphasis on differences between the various *madhāhib* and to obstinate adherence to trivialities within them, which in turn gradually incite the modernist and traditionalist 'reformers' and their followers to attack falsely the *mujtahidūn*, thereby undermining legitimate authority, and to discredit the concept and validity of the *madhhab* in Islamic life. The false *'ulamā'* are not able to develop the interpretations of the *mujtahidūn* along their proper courses within the clear guidelines, and their incessant elaboration of trivialities leads to the neglect of the real problem of education. They are content at leaving the Muslims' basic education in *farḍu 'ayn* knowledge at the infantile level while they allow the development of *farḍu kifāyah* knowledge to increase tremendously. In this way the amount of secular knowledge increases and develops in the Muslim's life out of proportion to the religious, so that the Muslim spends most of his adult life knowing more about the world and less about religion. Thus we have weak Muslims and weak and dangerous leaders whose comprehension and knowledge of Islām is stunted at the level of immaturity; and because of this Islām itself is erroneously made to appear as if 'undeveloped' or 'misdeveloped' or left to 'stagnate'. The increase in *farḍu kifāyah* knowledge and preoccupation in emphasizing its role in life without due emphasis on its acquisition being organized in proportionate balance with that of the *farḍu 'ayn* at all levels of education naturally directs the attention solely to the problems of state and society, for the state and the society are the true referents in respect of the *farḍu kifāyah*. The preoccupation in our age with the Islamic state and the *ummah* is succinct indication of the preponderant estimation accorded to the acquisition of *farḍu kifāyah* knowledge. In this respect, too, the social, political, and legal sciences in that category of knowledge has been demanding — and receiving — undue attention and ascendancy over the other category in our estimation and our consciousness. It is easy to see why, under these circumstances, the trend of affairs in Muslim life leads to the 'socialization' of Islām; and the levelling of the Holy Prophet, upon whom be Peace, to the same level as the masses is but a logical consequence of that 'socialization'. Together with 'socialization', rationalism—the kind understood in the West, that is, as derived from the concept *ratio*, not the kind we mean as derived from the Quranic '*aql* — is advocated by the 'modernists' who emulate the example of their predecessors at the turn of the century. They futilely attempt to 'rationalize' Verses of the Holy Qur'ān they find convenient to their purpose in line with the theories and findings of modern science. Their habit, however, is to remain silent on many of the other Verses which in fact cannot be so fathomed and which prove their thinking to be inadequate and confused. They likewise rationalize all episodes in the life of the Holy Prophet, upon whom be Peace, and present them in a 'despiritualized' version. By ineptly treating the nature of revelation as if it were a 'natural' phenomenon, and the Holy Qur'ān as if it were created and on the same level as other books; by presumptuously 'despiritualizing' the life and person of the Holy Prophet, upon whom be Peace, they prepare the ground for a 'secularized' Islām. They draw inspiration about ideas on state and society and man not so much from Islām and Islamic sources as from Western European sources about liberty, equality, and fraternity; about the social contract and the doctrine of human rights and humanistic individualism. The successes of socialism in the West in recent times have blindly encouraged their thinking in identifying socialism with Islām — at least as a political theory and social order—as if the choice of life-style open to Muslims lies solely between capitalism and socialism! They do not see that Islām is neither the one nor the other. If they had so seen, then they ought to have thought out their ideas about state and society and man based on their own intellectual and original efforts grounded upon Islām and the Islamic sources in the manner of the *mujtahidūn* of old. But they are intellectually lazy, or inadequate, or incapable of original *ijtihād*, and prefer instead to let Western thinkers think and realize the ideas for them to appropriate conveniently and islamicize in slip-shod fashion. They do this not only at the theoretical level in the socio-political and socio-economic spheres of life, but at the practical level as well, in which the educational, economic, financial, legal and other aspects of societal life are being likewise involved. They are, curiously enough, the very ones who clamour for *ijtihād* while in fact not even one fulfills the conditions for being a *mujtahid*! The 'traditionalists', although not necessarily in agreement with the 'modernists' in all respects in what they think and say and advocate, are nevertheless influenced by them and are infected by the same disease of socializing and despiritualizing Islām and levelling all Muslims. They are, unwittingly perhaps, aiding the process of 'secularizing' Islām in attempting to suppress its intellectual and spiritual elements. They and the 'modernists' erroneously blame *taṣawwuf* in particular as the cause of the degeneration of Muslims. In reality, however, they possess neither the intellectual capacity nor spiritual vision to understand *taṣawwuf*, and what they do not understand they condemn. They say ignorantly that *taṣawwuf* is alien to Islām, and that no matter how one looks at it *taṣawwuf* contains germs of decline and degeneration. They are blind to the fact that *taṣawwuf* is an integral part if Islām; that just as all reality and truth has an outer and inner aspect to it so is *taṣawwuf* the inner dimension of Islām; its sincere and correct practice is none other than the intensification of the *sharī'ah* upon one's self; it is the expression of *iḥsān* in the '*abd*; it is *'ibādah* fortified and enlightened by intellectual discernment leading to spiritual apprehension of realities; it is the practice of the *sharī'ah* at the station of *iḥsān*; it is established upon certainty as it is based upon *ḥikmah* and *al-'ilm al-ladunniyy* — wisdom and spiritual knowledge which God grants to whomsoever he pleases of the elect among His servants. It is also knowledge that enables the possessor to recognize and acknowledge the hierarchical order (*marātib*) of reality and truth, and so it is the fount of true *adab*. Its technical vocabulary is derived from its chief Source, the Holy Qur'ān, and its interpretation and practice is grounded upon the Sunnah. Its exponents are the saints, the *awliyā'*, the Friends of God. To say as they do that *taṣawwuf* contains germs of decline and degeneration is to imply that its Sources and vital principles, the Holy Qur'ān and the Sunnah, are the repository of those very germs! The germs of decline and degeneration are contained not in *taṣawwuf* and its sublime Sources, but in the ignorant who misunderstands, misapplies and commits malpractices leading to all sorts of aberrations and excesses. If they who condemn *taṣawwuf* mean by it the aberrations and excesses perpetrated by the ignorant, then they should say so and clearly distinguish the true from the false, and *condemn the false*. But just as they attack the *mujtahidūn* because they see them through the trivialities projected by the *'ulamā'* of less authoritative worth and by those who are even less so, in the same way they condemn *taṣawwuf* because they see it through the aberrant and excessive mind of the ignorant who falsely claim to be its exponents. They seem to fall into the habit of seeing what they think is the true through the eyes of the false, and so see not the true in reality; and seeing in this fashion they assume the self-styled task of 'purifying' Islām from what they falsely see to be stains of impurity. *Taṣawwuf* as seen by them is such a stain. In their method they are like people who see stains on a white wall and who, wishing to cleanse the wall of the stains, employ too much detergent, and of the wrong kind withal, so that instead of erasing the stains only they erase part of the whiteness of the wall as well and so disfigure the whole wall. If we cast a cursory glance at Muslim history we must see that *taṣawwuf* is not the cause of Muslim decline and degeneration. The loss of *adab* in the sense we have explained is the real perpetrator of decline and degeneration among us. Not only have the *'ulamā'* of less authoritative worth and those who are downright false, having undermined the authority of the great, neglected to inculcate correct knowledge of Islām and its world view in the Muslim mind through systematic organization of knowledge in structured educational formula but, to add to the general confusion and ignorance that such neglect entails, the rulers among Muslims have contributed significantly to the chaos. Like the false *'ulamā'* taking delight in endless controversy, in disputations and polemics and in hurling the accusation of unbelief against each other, the rulers take prime delight in endless struggle and warfare destructive to all. A classic example is Timūr who instead of conquering Russia and China, a feat which he was well able to accomplish and which would perhaps have altered the course of world history for the better, turned against the Persians and the Turks and the Egyptians and wrought havoc and devastation among fellow Muslims. In the history of the *Ahl al-Taṣawwuf*, the *ṭarīqah* came into existence in the 13th century after many turbulent periods of Muslim history. The degeneration among the *Ahl al-Ṭarīqah* came after the 15th century. Such degeneration is not to be construed as the cause, but as the effect of the decline and degeneration already begun in earlier centuries due to the loss of *adab*. *Taṣawwuf* proper has strengthened the belief and faith of Muslims in ages of tyranny and confusion; it has inculcated *adab*, and has adorned our civilization and our souls with the gift of incomparably rich and lofty spiritual literature from which we might derive the important bases for the education of the individual Muslim. The *taṣawwuf* that they blame, then, is not the *taṣawwuf* that the *Ahl al-Taṣawwuf* know, and it is therefore not *taṣawwuf*, and the blame is not to be laid on *taṣawwuf*. Rather it is neglect in developing and formulating a systematic educational programme based on Islamic principles already clarified by the great interpreters of Islām—neglect in implementing a coordinated, unified system of education developed out of the intellectual and spiritual vision of men of discernment, in pursuit of incessant jurisprudential and political dissensions instead, spurred on by the emergence and spread of alien doctrines which sought to undermine the teachings of Islām from within, and which altogether arose out of the confusion in knowledge of Islām and the loss of *adab*, that is the cause of the degeneration and decline of Muslims. This cause is perpetuated in our time by the modernist 'reformers' who derive their inspiration partly from the West and partly from the *'ulamā'* of less authoritative worth, and by the traditionalist 'reformers' who derive their inspiration partly from the modernists and partly from the same line of lesser *'ulamā'*. Apart from their respective followers all over the Muslim world reflecting their leaders in various degrees of ignorance and arrogance, there is now a third group which I will call the secular scholars and intellectuals among the Muslims.

The secular scholars and intellectuals among the Muslims derive their inspiration mainly from the West. Ideologically they belong to the same line of descent as the modernist 'reformers' and their followers; and some of them cleave to the views of the traditionalist 'reformers' and their followers. The majority of them do not possess the intellectual, spiritual, and linguistic prerequisites of Islamic knowledge and epistemology so that they are severed from the cognitive and methodological approaches to the original sources of Islām and Islamic learning. In this way their knowledge of Islām is at the barest minimal level. Because they occupy a strategic position in the midst of the Community, and unless they drastically change their ways of thinking and believing, they pose a grave danger to the Islamic welfare of the Community. Of those who suffer from loss of *adab*, they are the most bold and insolent. The great *'ulamā'* of Islām, the men of intellectual and spiritual discernment and virtue, the savants, saints, and sages, are still talking to us through their works; teaching and admonishing and guiding us; interpreting and clarifying for us the Sources of Islām, and clearing away the obstacles along the Path to the Truth and right conduct so that we might achieve success in this world and in the next—and yet, because they no longer understand the meanings of those words of wisdom, the secular scholars and intellectuals among us refuse to listen and pay attention, but hang instead upon every word taught by their Western masters in the various branches of knowledge of the sciences, particularly in that branch known as the human sciences. They are like sons who while their good and wise fathers are seriously talking to them, stop their ears in heedlessness, and yet eagerly lend their ears to the words of strangers. They have no *adab*, for they do not recognize and acknowledge the legitimate authorities in the true hierarchical order, and they demonstrate by example and teach and advocate confusion and error. Their chief error is the levelling of the categories of knowledge in Islām, that is, the *farḍu 'ayn* and the *farḍu kifāyah*, so that there is now confusion as to which is which, in that the nature of *farḍu 'ayn* knowledge and its method of approach is confused with that of the *farḍu kifāyah*. In this way they emulate the ways of thinking and believing of Western man, and advocate such ways to their students in all spheres of life. Now, the West does not recognize and acknowledge *farḍu 'ayn* knowledge as it does not even possess or know of any other category of knowledge except that which we have designated as *farḍu kifāyah*. This is in fact the main reason why, as demonstrated in the course of Western intellectual history throughout the ages and the rise of secular philosophy and science in Western civilization, the Western conception of knowledge based upon its experience and consciousness must invariably lead to secularization. There can be no doubt, therefore, that if the secular Muslim scholars and intellectuals allow themselves and are allowed to confuse the Muslim youth in knowledge, the deislamization of the Muslim mind will continue to take effect with greater persistence and intensity, and will follow the same kind of secularizing course in future generations. Large numbers among them do not fully understand the nature of Western culture and civilization whence they draw their inspiration and toward which they stand agape in reverential awe and servile humility portraying the attitude of the inferior. They do not even completely grasp the contents and implications of the teachings of their alien masters, being content only to repeat them in vulgarized versions and so cheat the Muslim audience of their true worth. The best specimen of this breed among the tribes that possess no *adab* is to be found in abundance in Malaysia and Indonesia where systematic deislamization has been implemented since colonial days, and where the momentum of secularization is more pronounced than in other parts of the Muslim world. Here perhaps, in this predominantly Islamic region of Southeast Asia, the loss of *adab* due to ignorance of Islām and its world view, as a religion and a civilization, is at a more advanced stage than elsewhere in the Muslim world particularly among the secular Muslim scholars and intellectuals. This state of affairs is due partly to the fact that the process of islamization began to take effect at a relatively later date than in other Muslim regions, and that islamization has been interrupted by the arrival of Western colonialism and cultural imperialism. Moreover, the bulk of the *'ulamā'* are equally immersed in loss of *adab*, seeing that they are the blind followers of the modernists as well as the traditionalists. In deislamizing the Muslims, the Western administrators and colonial theorists have first severed the pedagogical connection between the Holy Qur'ān and the local language by establishing a system of secular education where race and traditional culture are emphasized. At the higher levels linguistics and anthropology are introduced as the methodological tools for the study of language and culture, and Western values and models and orientalist scholarship and philology for the study of literature and history. Then, still being brought to bear upon the study of language and literature—which are the identifying and consolidating cultural elements of islamization—and of history and traditional culture, sociology and educational theory and psychology are significantly introduced. These misplaced at the purely rational disposal of scholars and intellectuals inadequately equipped with knowledge of Islām and its worldview tend to reduce Islām to the level of other religions as if it were the proper subject of the philosophy and the sociology of religion, and as if it were an evolved and developed expression of primitive religion. And all these and other fields of knowledge in the human sciences, including those philosophical elements in the theoretical aspects of the natural, physical and biological sciences, instilled into the marginal minds of the secular Muslim scholars and intellectuals are such that their knowledge so conceived is productive not only of potential and theoretical confusion, but also of actual and practical error as well. Through the unbalanced assimilation and imparting of such knowledge without any islamizing science and judgement being brought to bear upon its every proposition, and the active participation in its formulation and dissemination by the secular scholars and intellectuals, the rapid propagation of loss of *adab* is assured and indeed becomes a widespread reality. These false leaders among Muslims are responsible for causing the romanization of the originally Arabic script of the language, facilitating gradual severance from its formal, lexical and conceptual connections with the Sources of Islām, with their own Islamic sources and with the languages of the other Muslim peoples; for causing the dearabization, westernization and confusion of the language and its semantic and general vocabulary so that many important concepts pertaining to Islām and the Islamic world view have lost their transparency and have become opaque; for causing the emergence of the journal and the newspaper—so significantly unislamic in concept and purpose—and of mediocre journalists and writers of rustic quality who all contribute to the mutilation of the standards of literary values and expression established by Islām; for causing the widespread emergence of the marginal Muslim and the marginal society stranger to the *ummah*, and hence for causing the disintegration of consciousness in the ummatic solidarity; for causing the severance of the Muslim past from the consciousness of the present; for causing the establishment in our midst of an educational system designed, from the lowest to the highest levels, to perpetuate the secular ideology; for causing the rise of various forms of chauvinism and socialism; for reviving the Jāhilī spirit of advocating a return to preislamic values and cultural tradition—and many more which for obvious reasons it is not necessary to detail here. And the same is true, in varying degrees of absence of *adab* and in respect of their character traits, their quality, their contagious contribution to error and confusion in knowledge of Islām and its worldview and their propagation of false knowledge, of other such scholars and intellectuals among the Muslims wherever they might be in the Muslim world and whether in the Arabic speaking regions or not. They all have become conscious or unconscious agents of Western culture and civilization, and in this capacity they represent what we have earlier identified as the external sources and causes of our dilemma. But their existence amongst us as part of the Community creates for us the situation whereby what was once regarded as 'external' has now moved in methodically and systematically to become *internal.* In their present condition, they pose as the external menace which has become a grave internal problem, for intellectually, as it were, the *dār al-ḥarb* has advanced into the *dār al-islām;* they have become the enemy within, and—unlike the kinds known to the Muslims of the past—they are not hidden nor any longer lurking underground, but have surfaced in multitudes into the full light of awareness, advertising themselves openly and conspicuously and exhibiting their learned confusion and arrogant individualism so publicly that it is no longer possible to ignore them. The epistemological weapons they use to bring about the deislamization of the Muslim mind are invariably the same, and these are — apart from the underlying principles of secular philosophy and science that produced and nurtured them — anthropology, sociology, linguistics, psychology and the principles and methods of education. If the underlying principles and methods of these sciences are not made subject to some kind of islamizing formula whereby they would be rendered harmless, then, as they are, they would continue to be harmful to the Islamic welfare of the Community.

Loss of *adab*, then, not only implies loss of knowledge; it means also loss of the capacity and ability to recognize and acknowledge true leaders.[111] If all are levelled to the level of the masses, the *'awāmm*, how can true leaders stand out above the rest? If true leaders are denied their rightful place above those they lead, how can they be recognized and acknowledged by the led? And true leaders must not be confused with the false, for how can nightingales, put in the same cage as crows, sing? To put true leaders in lofty stations in our estimation and to put ourselves below them and to revere, to love, to respect, to affirm their veracity and confirm in our actions their wise counsels and learned teachings in humility is not to *worship* them, as the narrow-minded among the modernist and traditionalist 'reformers' erroneously think. Were the Angels worshipping Ādam, upon whom be Peace, when they prostrated themselves before him? Indeed, they were obeying God, Glorious and Exalted, and recognizing and acknowledging the superior knowledge bestowed upon the first man by his Creator — they not only saw the clay he is made from, but they recognized and acknowledged even more so the spirit that God breathed into him. It was Iblīs who saw only the clay and refused to recognize and acknowledge Ādam's superior nature, and disdained to

---

111 This, then is the reason why Muslims today often raise the question as posed on p. 109 above; it is only at this stage that the answer to that question can be clearly understood and appreciated.

prostrate before him in spite of the Divine Command. Recognition and acknowledgement of excellence in another does not mean to regard the other as a *rabb* and to assume an attitude of the *'abd* towards that other; it is no other than to recognize and acknowledge God's Knowledge and Will and Power and Just Purpose, His Bounty, Charity and Love in bestowing excellence in one over the other, so that that one might share it with others. But only those others who recognize and acknowledge derive benefit from it, not those who do not.

I have in this chapter briefly summarized the various sources and natures of the problems that create our present general dilemma, and have identified and isolated the main, over-riding crisis so that we might understand and know its cause and be able to take the right steps in preparing a real and all-curing remedy.

We must see that the three main groups that perpetuate loss of *adab* in our times, and that not only perpetuate, but also consolidate its paralyzing influence and intensify its odious spread among the generations of contemporary Muslims, are not in reality our true leaders. Without knowing any of them, and without being in any way guided by them, we can still know about Islām and its world view from the great *'ulamā* of the past who are the real interpreters of the Sources of such knowledge. Conversely, without knowing the true teachers of the past and without being guided by them, it is almost impossible to arrive at the correct understanding and knowledge of Islām and its world view. It were as if the false leaders of our times have been fashioned in the mould of the crafty Master Magician in the guise of new lamps meant to be traded for the old. They indeed claim to be the new lamps; and we must not fall into the error of the ignorant wife of Aladdin, trading the old for the new, unaware of the priceless value and wonderful quality of the old far surpassing all of the new put together. The thinking and methods and example adopted by these false leaders and their followers, compounded of a mixture of truth and falsehood and right and wrong which are the ingredients of confusion, propagated and advocated at a time when Muslims are already confused and desperate and in no balanced state of mind and spirit to absorb more confusion, have effected among the generality who are influenced by them a warped understanding of Islām and a clouded vision of its interpretation of the world and of reality and truth. The effect of their teachings among the generality of Muslims, particularly the younger generation who are experiencing the effects of westernization, is the tendency towards a relentless and erroneous attitude of levelling by which they judge all things. Their words and actions betray their mental and attitudinal condition of levelling in which they imply and even understand the Holy Qur'ān to be on the same level as other books; Islām to be on the same level as other religions; the Holy Prophet, upon whom be Peace, to be on the same level as other Prophets, Peace be upon them all, who all are regarded as being on the same level as ordinary men; the knowledge to be on the same level as other sciences; true leaders to be on the same level as false ones, and the greater to be on the same level as the lesser; the life of the world to be on the same level of importance as that of the hereafter. It is this levelling of all instilled into the understanding of the masses without due consideration given to the quality of that understanding, and without due elaboration as to the distinctions that naturally exist in the hierarchical order of creation, especially in the human order, that is productive of the 'socialization' of Islām. The despiritualization of man, starting from the Holy Prophet himself—the despiritualization that must necessarily take place as a precondition to the levelling process—tends to involve Islām absurdly in a kind of secularization. These groups of false leaders, who are not even sure as to what they are supposed to do, and are equally groping for solutions to general problems we encounter today—solutions hastily conceived in piecemeal fashion, of tentative validity and dubious soundness—have indeed misrepresented the achievements of the truly great ' *ulamā* of the past: the *mujtahidūn,* the men of piety and virtue and of intellectual and spiritual excellence, in connection with their interpretation of Islām and its world view. Inclined as they are to see only small matters and not great ones in their estimation of superiors, they have not understood those men completely and have misrepresented them in caricature before us. Our task ahead is to represent the true leaders of the past in truer light, to exercise justice in our estimation of them from whom our predecessors derived guidance and knowledge. We must reexamine the misrepresentations, referring every detail to the original sources they allegedly claim to represent; we must scrutinize their premises, their deductions and conclusions, and retrace the paths of their logic to see how far they have been correct or have been led astray by their own process of inadequate thinking; we must ourselves know the originals and understand them in their correct perspectives. It is our duty to diligently study the thoughts of the true leaders of the part, who were all recognized and acknowledged by a grateful Community; who all served Islām and the Muslims with signal merit, recognized and acknowledged by a *knowing* Community of contemporaries without their true characters and qualities having to be fabricated and 'built up' long after they were gone, as so often happens in our age of falsehood and confusion. We must learn from the great of the past their knowledge and wisdom. This does not mean that we ourselves cannot contribute any further knowledge that can be contributed, but it does mean that we must first draw our strength the inspiration from their wisdom and knowledge, and that when we do begin to contribute ours, we must recognize and acknowledge them as our teachers, and not disparage and denounce, for *ijtihād* can be exercised without having to undermine legitimate authority. They are like torches that light the way along difficult paths; when we have such torches to light our way, of what use are mere candles?

V

THE DEWESTERNIZATION
OF KNOWLEDGE

Introduction

Many challenges have arisen in the midst of man's confusion throughout the ages, but none perhaps more serious and destructive to man than today's challenge posed by Western civilization. I venture to maintain that the greatest challenge that has surreptitiously arisen in our age is the challenge of knowledge, indeed, not as against ignorance; but knowledge as conceived and disseminated throughout the world by Western civilization; knowledge whose nature has become problematic because it has lost its true purpose due to being unjustly conceived, and has thus brought about chaos in man's life instead of, and rather than, peace and justice; knowledge which pretends to be real but which is productive of confusion and scepticism, which has elevated doubt and conjecture to the 'scientific' rank in methodology and which regards doubt as an eminently valid epistemological tool in the pursuit of truth; knowledge which has, for the first time in history, brought chaos to the Three Kingdoms of Nature; the animal, vegetal and mineral. It seems to me important to emphasize that knowledge is not neutral, and can indeed be infused with a nature and content which masquerades as knowledge. Yet it is in fact, taken as a whole, not true knowledge, but its interpretation through the prism, as it were, the worldview, the intellectual vision and psychological perception of the civilization that now plays the key

133

role in its formulation and dissemination. What is formulated and disseminated is knowledge infused with the character and personality of that civilization — knowledge presented and conveyed as knowledge in that guise so subtly fused together with the real so that others take it unawares *in toto* to be the real knowledge *per se*. What is the character and personality, the essence and spirit of Western civilization that has so transformed both itself and the world, bringing all who accept its interpretation of knowledge to a state of chaos leading to the brink of disaster? By 'Western civilization' I mean the civilization that has evolved out of the historical fusion of cultures, philosophies, values and aspirations of ancient Greece and Rome; their amalgamation with Judaism and Christianity, and their further development and formation by the Latin, Germanic, Celtic and Nordic peoples. From ancient Greece is derived the philosophical and epistemological elements and the foundations of education and of ethics and aesthetics; from Rome the elements of law and statecraft and government; from Judaism and Christianity the elements of religious faith; and from the Latin, Germanic, Celtic and Nordic peoples their independent and national spirit and traditional values, and the development and advancement of the natural and physical sciences and technology which they, together with the Slavic peoples, have pushed to such pinnacles of power. Islam too has made very significant contributions to Western civilization in the sphere of knowledge and in the inculcation of the rational and scientific spirit, but the knowledge and the rational and scientific spirit have been recast and remoulded to fit the crucible of Western culture so that they have become fused and amalgamated with all the other elements that form the character and personality of Western civilization. But the fusion and amalgamation thus evolved produced a characteristic dualism in the world view and values of Western culture and civilization; a dualism that cannot be resolved into a harmonious unity, for it is formed of conflicting ideas, values, cultures, beliefs, philosophies, dogmas, doctrines and theologies altogether reflecting an all-pervasive dualistic vision of reality and truth locked in despairing combat. Dualism abides in all aspects of Western life and philosophy: the speculative, the social, the political, the cultural — just as it pervades with equal inexorableness the Western religion.

In formulates its vision of truth and reality not upon revealed knowledge and religious belief, but rather upon cultural tradition reinforced by strictly philosophical premises based upon speculations pertaining mainly to secular life centered upon man as physical entity and rational animal, setting great store upon man's rational capacity alone to unravel the mysteries of his total environment and involvement in existence, and to conceive out of the results of speculations based upon such premises his evolutionary ethical and moral values to guide and order his life accordingly. There can be no certainty in philosophical speculations in the sense of religious certainty based on revealed knowledge understood and experienced in Islam;[112] and because of this the knowledge and values that project the worldview and direct the life of such a civilization are subject to constant review and change.

The inquiring spirit of Western culture and civilization

---

112 See above, p. 86, reference to *yaqīn* (certainty). The Holy Qur'ān mentions three degrees or levels of certainty of knowledge: certainty derived by inference, whether deductive or inductive: *'ilm al-yaqīn* (*al-Takāthur* (102): 5); certainty derived by direct vision: *'ayn al-yaqīn* (*al-Takāthur* (102): 7); certainty derived by direct experience *ḥaqq al-yaqīn* (*al-Ḥāqqah* (69): 51). These levels of certain knowledge pertain to truth, whether manifest or hidden, empirical or transcendental; and the certain knowledge of what is hidden has the same force of certainty as that of what is visible. These levels of certainty also pertain to that which is perceived by the spiritual organ of cognition, the heart (*al-qalb*),and refers to knowledge as belief and faith (*īmān*). See p. 75 above.

originated with disenchantment towards religion as that civilization understands it. Religion in the sense we mean, as *dīn*, has never really taken root in Western civilization due to its excessive and misguided love of the world and secular life and of man and preoccupation with man's secular destiny. Its inquiring spirit is basically generated in a state of doubt and inner tension; the inner tension is the result of the clash of conflicting elements and opposing values in the sustained dualism, while the doubts maintain the state of inner tension. The state of inner tension in turn produces the insatiable desire to seek and to embark on a perpetual journey of discoveries.

The quest insatiable and the journey perpetual because doubt ever prevails, so that what is sought is never really found, what is discovered never really satisfies its true purpose. It is like the thirsty traveller who at first sincerely sought the water of knowledge, but who later, having found it plain perhaps, proceeded to temper his cup with the salt of doubt so that his thirst now becomes insatiable though he drinks incessantly, and that in thus drinking the water that cannot slake his thirst, he has forgotten the original and true purpose for which the water was sought.

The fundamental truths of religion are regarded, in such a scheme of things, as mere theories, or discarded altogether as futile illusions. Absolute values are denied and relative values affirmed; nothing can be certain, except the certainty that nothing can be certain. The logical consequence of such an attitude towards knowledge, which determines and is determined by the world view, is to negate God and the Hereafter and affirm man and his world. Man is deified and Deity humanized, and the world becomes man's sole preoccupation so that even his own immortality consists in the continuation of his species and his culture in this world. What is called 'change' and 'development' and 'progress' in all their aspects as far as Western civilization is concerned is the result of the insatiable quest and perpetual journey spurred on by doubt and inner tension. The context in which the notions of change and development and progress is understood is always this-worldy, presenting a consistently materialistic world view that can be termed as a kind of humanistic existentialism. The spirit of Western culture that describes itself as Promethean is like the Camusian Sisyphus who desperately hopes that all is well. I say *desperately hopes* that all is well because I suspect that the fact cannot be that all is well, for I believe that he can never really be truly happy in that state. The pursuit of knowledge, like the struggle to push the Stone from the plains up the Mountain where at the top it is destined to roll down again, becomes a kind of serious *game,* never ceasing, as if to distract the soul from the *tragedy* of unattainment. No wonder, then, that in Western culture tragedy is extolled as being among the noblest values in the *drama* of human existence!

Reliance upon the powers of human reason alone to guide man through life; adherence to the validity of the dualistic vision of reality and truth; affirmation of the reality of the evanescent-aspect of existence projecting a secular worldview; espousal of the doctrine of humanism; emulation of the allegedly universal reality of drama and tragedy in the spiritual, or transcendental, or inner life of man, making drama and tragedy real and dominant elements in human nature and existence — these elements altogether taken as a whole, are, in my opinion, what cons- titute the substance, the spirit, the character and per- sonality of Western culture and civilization. It is these ele- ments that determine for that culture and civilization the moulding of its concept of knowledge and the direction of its purpose, the formulation of its contents and the systematization of its dissemination; so that the knowledge that is now systematically disseminated throughout the world is not necessarily *true* knowledge, but that which is imbued with the character and personality of Western culture and civilization, and charged with its spirit and geared to its purpose. And it is these elements, then, that must be identified and separated and isolated from the body of knowledge, so that knowledge may be distinguished from what is imbued with these elements, for these elements and what is imbued with them do not represent knowledge as such but they only determine the characteristic form in which knowledge is conceived and evaluated and interpreted in accordance with the purpose aligned to the worldview of Western civilization. It follows too that apart from the identification and separation and isolation of these elements from the body of knowledge, which will no doubt also alter the conceptual forms and values and interpretation of some of the contents of knowledge as it is now presented,[113] its very purpose and system of deployment and dissemination in institutions of learning and in the domain of education must needs be altered accordingly. It may be argued that what is suggested is but *another, alternative* interpretation of knowledge imbued with other conceptual forms and values aligned to another purpose which reflects another world view; and that this being so, and by the same token, what is formulated and disseminated as knowledge might not necessarily reflect *true* knowledge. This, however, remains to be seen, for the test of true knowledge is in man himself, in that if, through an alternative interpretation of knowledge man knows himself and his ultimate destiny,[114] and in thus knowing he achieves happiness,[115] then that knowledge, in spite of its being imbued with certain elements that determine the characteristic form in which it is conceived and evaluated and interpreted in accordance with the purpose aligned to a particular world view, is true knowledge; for such knowledge has fulfilled man's purpose for knowing.[116]

---

113 'Some of the contents of knowledge' referred to here pertains mainly to the human sciences
114 See above, pp. 75-85; 89-95.
115 See above, pp. 74-75.
116 For a decisive answer to the above argument, see below, what is referred to by note 124.

The nature of man

Man has a dual nature, he is both soul and body, he is at once physical being and spirit (15: 29; 23: 12-14).[117] God taught him the names (*al-asmā'*) of everything (2: 31), By 'the names' we infer that it means the knowledge (*al-'ilm*) of everything (*al-ashyā'*). This knowledge does not refer to knowledge of the essence (*dhāt*) or inmost ground (*sirr*) of a thing (*shay'*) such as, for example, the spirit (*al-rūḥ*), of which only a little knowledge is vouchsafed to man by God (17:85); it refers to knowledge of accidents (sing. *'araḍ*) and attributes (sing *ṣifah*) pertaining to things sensible and intelligible (*maḥsūsāt* and *ma'qūlāt*) so as to make known the relations and distinctions existing between them and to clarify their natures within these contexts in order to discern and understand their causes, uses, and specific individual purpose. Man is also given knowledge about (*ma'rifah*) God, His Absolute Oneness; that God is his true Lord (*rabb*) and true Object of Worship (*ilāh*) (7: 172; 3: 18). The seat of this knowledge in man, both *al-'ilm* and *ma'rifah*, is his spirit or soul (*al-nafs*) and his heart (*al-qalb*) and his intellect (*al-'aql*). In virtue of the fact that man knows (*'arafa*) God in His Absolute Oneness as his true Lord, such knowledge, and the necessary reality of the situation that follows from it, has bound man in a Covenant (*mīthāq, 'ahd*) determining his purpose and attitude and action with respect to himself and to God (*q. v.* 7: 172 fol.). This 'binding' and 'determining' of man to a Covenant with God and to a precise nature in regard to his purpose and attitude and action is the binding and determining in religion (*dīn*) and in real submission (*aslama*) respectively. Thus both *dīn* and *aslama* are mutual correlates in the nature of man (ref. *fiṭrah*). Man's purpose is to do *'ibādah* to God (51: 56), and his duty is obedience (*ṭā'ah*) to God, which conforms with his essential nature (*fiṭrah*) created

---

117 In this chapter numerals in brackets refer to the chapters and verses of the Holy Qur'ān; numerals preceding the colon refer to the former (i.e. *sūrah*) and those that come after to the latter (i.e. *āyah*).

for him by God (*q. v.* 30: 30). But man is also "composed of forgetfulness (*nisyān*);" and he is called *insān* basically precisely because, having testified to himself the truth of the Covenant, which enjoins obedience to God's Commands and Prohibitions, he *forgot* (*nasiya*) to fulfill his duty and purpose (*q. v.* narration from ibn 'Abbās:

انما سمى الانسان انسانا لانه عهد اليه فنسي

> Indeed, man is called *insān* because, having covenanted with Him, he forgot (*nasiya*).

with reference to 20: 115). Forgetfulness is the cause of man's disobedience, and this blameworthy nature inclines him towards injustice (*ẓulm*) and ignorance (*jahl*)(33: 72). But God has equipped him with the faculties of right vision and apprehension, of real savouring of truth and right speech and communication; and has indicated to him the right and the wrong with respect to the course of action he should take so that he might strive to attain his bright destiny (90: 8-10). The choice is left to him. Moreover, God has equipped him with intelligence to know right from wrong and truth from flasehood; and even though his intelligence might confuse him, and provided he is sincere and true to his real nature, God, out of His Bounty and Mercy and Grace will — as He Wills — bestow His Guidance (*hudā*) upon him to help him attain to truth and right conduct (*q. v.* the supreme example of the Prophet Ibrāhīm, upon whom be Peace!, in 6: 74-82). Man, thus equipped, is meant to be vicegerent (*khalīfah*) of God on earth (2: 30), and as such the weighty burden of trust (*amānah*) is placed upon him — the trust of responsibility to rule according to God's Will and Purpose and His Pleasure (33: 72). The *amānah* implies *responsibility* to be *just* to it; and the 'rule' refers not simply to ruling in the socio-political sense, nor to controlling nature in the scientific sense, but more fundamentally, in its encompassing of the concept *nature* (*ṭabī'ah*), it refers to the ruling, and governing, and controlling, and maintenance of man by his self. Man also has two souls (*nafsān*) analogous to his dual nature: the higher, rational soul (*al-nafs al-nāṭiqah*); and the lower, animal soul (*al-nafs al-ḥayawāniyyah*). When God proclaimed the reality of His Lordship to man it is the rational soul that He addressed, so that it is the rational soul that knows God. In order for man to fulfill his Covenant with God, to constantly confirm and affirm the Covenant within his total self so that it is enacted as action, as work (*'amal, i. e.* with reference to *'ibādah*) performed in obedience to God's Law (*i. e.* the *sharī'ah*), the rational soul must assert its supremacy and exert its power and rule over the animal soul, which is subject to it and which must be rendered submissive by it. The effective power and rule excercised by the rational soul over the animal soul is in fact *dīn;* and the conscious subjugation and total and willing submission of the latter to the former is none other than *aslama* and *islām.* Both *dīn* and *islām,* leading to excellence in religious conduct (*iḥsạn*), have to do with the freedom of the rational soul, which freedom means the power (*quwwah*) and capacity (*wus'*) to do justice to itself; and this in turn refers to excercise of its rule and supremacy and guidance and maintenace over the animal soul and body. The power and capacity to do justice to itself alludes to its constant affirmation and fulfillment of the Covenant it has sealed with God. *Justice* in Islām is not what refers to a state of affairs which can operate only within a two-person-relation or a dual-party-relation situation, such as: between one man and another; or between the society and the state; or between the king and his subjects. The man of Islām, the true Muslim, the *khalīfatu'Llāh,* is not bound by the social contract, nor does he espouse the doctrine of the Social Contract. Indeed, though he lives and works within the bounds of social polity and authority and contributes his share towards the social good, and though he behaves *as if* a social contract were in force, his is, nevertheless, an *individual contract* reflecting the Covenant his soul has sealed with God; for the Covenant is in reality made for *each* and *every individual* soul. The purpose and end of ethics in

Islām is ultimately for the individual; what the man of Islām does here he does in the way he believes to be good only because God and His Messenger say so and he trusts that his actions will find favour with God.[118]

We have described most cursorily the bare essentials relating to the nature of man, saying that he is, as it were, a 'double associate': possessed of a dual nature of soul and body, the soul rational and the body animal; that he is at once spirit and physical being, and that he has individuality referred to as the self; that he has attributes reflecting those of his Creator. We say specifically that he has knowledge of the names of things, and knowledge about God; that he has spiritual and rational organs of cognition such as the heart and the intellect; that he has faculties relating to physical, intellectual and spiritual vision and experience; that he has the potentiality to contain within his self guidance and wisdom, and that he has the power and capacity to do justice to his self. We also say that he is forgetful by nature and hence subject to disobedience, injustice and ignorance. In him both qualities, positive and negative, contend for supremacy; but in him also is sealed the means of salvation in true religion and submission. To sum up our brief exposition, we now say that man in his totality is the *locus* (*maḥall* or *makān*) in which *dīn* occurs, and as such he is like a city (*madīnah*), a state, a comopolis. In his real nature he is, as it were, the dweller in his self's city, citizen in his own miniature kingdom. The concept of man as a microcosmic representation (*'ālam saghīr*) of the macrocosmos (*al-'ālam al-kabīr*) is most important in relation to knowledge — which is his paramount attribute responsible

---

118 For an elaboration of the concepts of justice and injustice in Islām, and their relationship to the Covenant with God, which must at this stage be recollected, see above, pp. 75-79. The same applies here to the concept in Islām that the Covenant is in reality not a doctrine of 'social contract' and that 'happiness' is knowledge which is identified with justice. See above, pp.74-75.

for the effective establishment of the just order in his self,
his being and existence — and to the organization
instruction, inculcation and dissemination of knowledge in
his education, specifically with reference to the university,
as will be presently outlined.

The nature of knowledge
There have been many expositions on the nature of
knowledge in Islām more than in any other religion,
culture, and civilization, and this is no doubt due to the
preeminent position and paramount role accorded to *al-
'ilm* by God in the Holy Qur'ān. These expositions, though
apparently varying in substance, encompass the nature of
knowledge in its totality. There have been distinctions made
between God's Knowledge and the knowledge of man
about God, and religion, and the world, and things sensible
and intelligible; about spiritual knowledge and wisdom.
Thus, for example, knowledge has been understood to
mean the Holy Qurān; the Revealed Law (*sharī'ah*); the
Sunnah; Islām; Faith (*īmān*); Spiritual Knowledge (*'ilm al-
ladunniyy*), Wisdom (*ḥikmah*), and Gnosis (*ma'rifah*), also
generally referred to as Light; Thought; Science (specific
'ilm, to which the plural: *'ulūm* is applied); Education.
These expositions range from the earliest periods of Islām
to the seventh century after the *Hijrah*, and they include
works on exegeses and commentaries of the Holy Qurān;
commentaries of the *Ḥadīth* by the Compilers of the various
Ṣiḥāḥ; works of the Imams on law and jurisprudence, and
those of other foremost jurists specifically concerned with
the elucidation of knowledge and discernment; books on
knowledge written by various scholars, savants, sages and
saints among Sunnīs and Shī'īs; expositions by the
Mu'tazilah, the Mutakallimūn, the Falāsifah, the Ṣūfīs and
the 'Ulama' in general; lexicons and dictionaries of
technical terminologies in *taṣawwuf* and philosophy and

---

119 For a summary of the various ideas on knowledge expressed
   by Muslim thinkers covering the above periods, see al-

the arts or sciences (*al-funūn*) by various grammarians, philologists, scholars and men of letters; and in anthologies and other works connected with education and *belle-lettres*.[119] It is generally understood that knowledge requires no definition (*ḥadd*);[120] that the understanding of what the concept couched in the term *'ilm* means is naturally apprehended by man's knowledge of knowledge, for knowledge is one of his most important attributes, and what it is is already clear to him, so that it dispenses with the need for an explanation describing its specific nature. It is also generally accepted that knowledge can be classified into essential elements, so that its basic classification, insofar as man is concerned, is useful. All knowledge comes from God. For the purpose of classification for our action, we say that in the same manner that man is of a dual nature possessed of two souls, so is knowledge of two kinds: the one is food and life for the soul, and other is provision with which man might equip himself in the world in his pursuit of pragmatic ends. The first kind of knowledge is given by

---

Tahānawī; *Kashshāf iṣṭilāḥāt al-funūn*, the article on *'ilm*. Most of it is derived from data contained in the *al-Mawāqif* of 'Aḍud al Dīn al-Ījī, who made extensive use of al-Āmidī's *Abkar al-Afkār*.

120 There have been many attemps made by Muslim thinkers to define knowledge philosophically and epistemologically, the best definition — according to al-Āmidī in his work cited in note 119 and also in another work; the *Iḥkām fī uṣūl al-aḥkām* — was that made by Fakhr al-Dīn al-Rāzi. Ibn Ḥazm, and also al-Ghazālī in his *Maqaṣid al-Falāsifah*, have distinguished the meaning of definition as being of two types, one referring to a description of the nature of the object defined (*rasm*); and the other to a concise specification of the distinctive characteristic of the object defined (*ḥadd*). We are here, however, not concerned with a philosophical or epistemological definition of knowledge, but more with its general classification designed to be applied to a system of order and discipline in the educational system.

God through revelation to man; and this refers to the Holy Qur'ān. The Holy Qur'ān is the complete and final Revelation, so that it suffices for man's guidance and salvation; and there is no other knowledge — except based upon it and pointing to it — that can guide and save man. God, however, has never ceased to communicate with man, and out of His Grace, Bounty and Charity He may bestow the favour of specific spiritual knowledge and wisdom upon the elect among His servants — His 'friends' (*i. e.* the *awliyā*')- in proportion to their various degrees of *iḥsān* (*q. v.* 10: 62, 18: 65, 31: 12, 38: 20). The Holy Qur'ān is *the* knowledge *par excellence.* The Holy Prophet, who may God Bless and give Peace! — who received the Revelation and brought to man the Holy Qur'ān as it was revealed to him by God, who thus brought to man *the* knowledge, whose own life is the most excellent and perfect interpretation of the Holy Qur'ān so that his life becomes for man the focus of emulation and true guiding spirit — is knowledge of that first knowledge on account of his nature and mission ordained by God. Hence his *sunnah,* which is his manner of interpreting God's Law (*sharī'ah*) in daily life and practice, is also part of that knowledge. The *sharī'ah* is God's Law embodied in the Holy Qur'ān and manifested in word (*qawl*), model action (*fi'il*), and silent confirmation (*taqrīr*) in the *sunnah* which includes spiritual knowledge and wisdom. So then, the Holy Qur'ān, the *sunnah,* the *sharī'ah,* '*ilm al-ladunniyy* and *ḥikmah* are the essential elements of the first kind of knowledge. As regards the last mentioned — spiritual knowledge and wisdom — man can only receive this through his acts of worship and devotion, his acts of service to God (*'ibādāt*) which, depending upon God's Grace and his own latent spiritual power and capacity created by God to receive it, the man receives by direct insight or spiritual savouring (*dhawq*) and unveiling to his spiritual vision (*kashf*). This knowledge pertains to his self or soul, and such knowledge (*ma'rifah*) —· when experienced in true emulation of the *sharī'ah* — gives insight into knowledge of God, and for that reason is the highest knowledge. We are here alluding to knowledge at the level of *ihsān*, where *'ibādah* has reached, or rather, has become identified with *ma'rifah*. (*q. v.* 51: 56 with reference to *li ya'budūn* which means, according to the interpretation of ibn 'Abbās: *li ya'rifūn*).[121] Since such knowledge ultimately depends upon God's Grace and because it entails deeds and works of service to God as prerequisites to its possible attainment, it follows that for it to be received knowledge of the prerequisites becomes necessary; and this includes knowledge of the essentials of Islām (*islām—īmān—ihsān*), their principles (*arkān*), their meanings and purpose and correct understanding and implementation in everyday life and practice: every Muslim must have knowledge of those prerequisites; must understand the basic essentials of Islām and the Unity of God, His Essence and Attributes (*tawhīd*); must have knowledge of the Holy Qur'ān, the Prophet, upon whom be God's Blessings and Peace!, his life and *sunnah*, and practise the knowledge thus based in deeds and works of service to God so that every man of Islām be already in the initial stage of that first knowledge, that he be set ready on the Straight Path that leads to God. His further progress along the path of highest virtue (*ihsān*) will depend upon his own knowledge, his own intuitive and speculative power and capacity and performance and sincerity of purpose. The second kind of knowledge refers to knowledge of the sciences (*'ulūm*), and is acquired through experience and observation and research; it is discursive and deductive and it refers to objects of pragmatical value. The first kind of knowledge is given by God to man through direct relevation, and the second through speculation and rational effort of enquiry based on his experience of the sensible and intelligible. The first refers to knowledge of objective truths necessary for our guidance, and the second to knowledge of sensible and intelligible data acquired (*kasbi*) for our use and

---

121 See above, note 76.

understanding. From the point of view of man, both kinds of knowledge have to be acquired through conscious *action* (*'amal*), for there is no useful knowledge without action resulting from it; and there is no worthwhile action without knowledge. The first knowledge unveils the mystery of Being and Existence and reveals the true relationship between man's self and his Lord, and since for man such knowledge pertains to the ultimate purpose for knowing, it follows that knowledge of its prerequisites becomes the basis and essential foundation for knowledge of the second kind, for knowledge of the latter alone, without the guiding spirit of the former, cannot truly lead man in his life, but only confuses and confounds him and enmeshes him in the labyrinth of endless and purposeless seeking. We also perceive that there is a limit for man even to the first and highest knowledge; whereas no limit obtains in the second kind, so that the possibility of perpetual wandering spurred on by intellectual deception and self-delusion in constant doubt and curiosity is always real. The individual man must limit his individual quest for knowledge of the second kind to his own practical needs and suited to his nature and capacity, so that he may set both the knowledge and himself in their right places in relation to his real self and thus maintain a condition of justice. For this reason and in order to achieve justice as the end, Islām distinguishes the quest for the two kinds of knowledge, making the one for the attainment of knowledge of the prerequisites of the first obligatory to all Muslims (*farḍ'ayn*), and that of the other obligatory to some Muslims only (*farḍ kifāyah*), and the obligation for the latter can indeed be transferred to the former category in the case of those who deem themselves duty-bound to seek it for their self-improvement. The division in the obligatory quest for knowledge into two categories is itself a procedure of doing justice to knowledge and to man who seeks it, for *all* of the knowledge of the prerequisties of the first knowledge is good for man, whereas *not all* of the knowledge of the second kind is good for him, for the man who seeks that latter knowledge, which would bear considerable influence in determining his secular role and position as a citizen, might not necessarily be a *good* man. The concept of a 'good man' in Islām connotes not only that he must be 'good' in the general social sense understood, but that he must also first be good to his self, and not be unjust to it in the way we have explained, for if he were unjust to his self, how can he really be just to others? Thus we see that, for Islām, (a) knowledge includes faith and belief (*īmān*); and that (b) the purpose for seeking knowledge is to inculcate goodness or justice in man as *man* and *individual self,* and not merely in man as citizen or integral part of society: it is man's value as real man, as the dweller in his self's city, as citizen in his own microcosmic kingdom, as spirit, that is stressed, rather than his value as a physical entity measured in terms of the pragmatic or utilitarian sense of his usefulness to state and society and the world.

As the philosophical basis for the purpose and aims of education, and for the establishment of an integrated core-knowledge in the educational system, it seems to me important to recollect the essential character of the Islāmic vision of Reality.[122] In the same way that the Islamic vision of Reality is centred on Being, so is that Being viewed in Islām as a Hierarchy from the highest to the lowest. Within this context is also seen the relationship between man and the universe, his position in the order of Being and his analogical description as a microcosm reflecting the Macrocosm without the reverse being the case. Knowledge is also ordered hierarchically, and our task at present is to alter the system of education known to us — and in some cases to modify it — so that it patterns itself after the Islamic system of order and discipline.

---

122 The reference here is to the philosophical vision (*shuhūd*)˙ of Reality and to the Islamic concepts of change, development and progress, which derive from the worldview of Islām. See above, pp. 85-88.

Definition and aims of education
We have said that justice implies knowledge, which also means that knowledge is prior to justice. We have defined justice as a harmonious condition or state of affairs whereby every thing or being is in its right and proper place — such as the cosmos; or similarly, a state of equilibrium, whether it refers to things or living beings. We said further that with respect to man and in view of his dual nature justice is a condition and situation whereby he is in his right and proper place — the situation in relation to others, and the condition in relation to his self. Then we mentioned that the knowledge of the 'right place' for a thing or a being to be is wisdom. Wisdom is a God-given knowledge enabling the one in whom the knowledge subsists to apply the knowledge in such wise that it (*i. e.* the application or judgement) causes the occurrence of justice. Justice is then the existential condition of wisdom manifested in the sensibilia and intelligibilia and in the spiritual realm in respect of the two souls of man. The external manifestation of justice in life and society is none other than the occurrence within it of *adab*. I am using the concept (*ma'nā*) of *adab* here in the early sense of the term, before the innovations of the literary geniuses. *Adab* in the original basic sense is the *inviting to a banquet*. The idea of a *banquet* implies that the host is a man of *honour* and *prestige*, and that *many* people are present; that the people who are present are those who in the host's estimation are deserving of the honour of the invitation, and they are therefore people of refined qualities and upbringing who are expected to behave as befits their station, in speech, conduct and etiquette. In the same sense that the enjoyment of fine food in a banquet is greatly enhanced by noble and gracious company, and that the food be partaken of in accordance with the rules of refined conduct, behaviour and etiquette, so is knowledge to be extolled and enjoyed, and approached by means of conduct as befits its lofty nature. And this is why we said analogically that knowledge is the *food* and *life* of the soul. In virtue of this, *adab* also means to *discipline* the

mind and *soul*; it is acquisition of the *good qualities* and *attributes* of mind and soul; it is to *perform* the *correct* as against the erroneous *action*, of *right* as against wrong; it is the *preserving from disgrace*. The analogy of invitation to a banquest to partake of fine food, and to knowledge to imbue the intellect and soul with sustenance from it, is significantly and profoundly expressed in a *hadīth* narrated by ibn Mas'ūd, may God be well pleased with him!:

ان هذا القران مأ دبة الله في الارض

فتعلموا من مأ دبتة

Verily this Qur'ān is God's Banquet on earth, so learn throughly, then, from (or of) His Banquet.

The *Lisān al-'Arab* says that *ma'dabat* means *mad'āt* (I: 206: 2) so that the Holy Qur'ān is God's invitation to a spiritual banquet on earth, and we are exhorted to partake of it by means of acquiring real knowledge of it. Ultimately, real knowledge of it is the 'tasting of its true flavour' — and that is why we said earlier, with reference to the essential elements of the first kind of knowledge, that man receives spiritual knowledge and wisdom from God by direct insight or spiritual savouring (*dhawq*), the experience of which almost simultaneously unveils the reality and truth of the matter to his spiritual vision (*kashf*). He in whom *adab* inheres reflects widsom; and with respect to society *adab* is the deployment of the just order within it. *Adab*, then, is the spectacle (*mashhad*) of justice as it is reflected by wisdom; and it is the recognition and acknowledgement of the various hierarchies (*marātib*) in the order of being and existence and knowledge, and concomitant action in accord with the recognition and acknowledgement. We have said earlier that the purpose for seeking knowledge in Islām is to inculcate goodness or justice in man as man and individual self. The aim of education in Islām is therefore to produce a good man. What is meant by 'good' in our concept of 'good man'? The fundamental element inhe-

rent in the Islamic concept of education is the inculcation
of *adab*, for it is *adab* in the all-inclusive sense here meant as
encompassing the spiritual and material life of man that
instills the quality of goodness that is sought after. *Education*
is precisely what the Prophet, upon whom be Peace, meant
by *adab* when he said:

اد بني ربي فاحسن تأ ديبي

My Lord educated (*addaba*) me, and made my education (*ta'dīb*) most excellent.

---

123 On the definition and a more extended elaboration of the
    concept of *adab*, see chapter IV, which treats of the subject.
    What is here proposed,that 'education' means *ta'dīb*, in
    contradistinction with the generally accepted *tarbiyah*, is of
    paramount importance and must seriously be considered.
    Tarbiyah in my opinion is a comparatively recent term
    applied to denote 'education'. Semantically, however, the
    term seems neither appropriate nor adequate in conveying
    the conception of education, which is peculiar only to man.
    Basically *tarbiyah* conveys the meaning of 'to nurture', 'to
    bear', 'to feed, foster, nourish, to cause to increase in
    growth', 'to rear', 'to bring forth mature produce,' 'to do-
    mesticate'. Its application in the Arabic language is not
    restricted to man alone, and its semantic fields extend to
    other species: to minerals, plants and animals; one can refer
    to cattle farming and stockbreeding, chicken farming and
    poultry husbandry, pisciculture and plant cultivation each as
    a form of *tarbiyah* respectively. Education is something pecu-
    liar only to man; and the activity involved and qualitative
    elements inherent in education are not the same as those
    involved and inherent in *tarbiyah*. Moreover, *tarbiyah* basically
    also refers to the idea of possession, and it is usually the
    'possessor' who exercises *tarbiyah* on the objects of *tarbiyah*.
    God, the Sustainer, Nourisher, Cherisher, Lord and Posses-
    sor of all (*al-rabb*) is *already* ever exercising His Dominion
    over all, so that *tarbiyah* is something that *man* must do. In
    the case of man it is usually the parents who exercise *tarbiyah*
    over their offspring. When the exercise of *tarbiyah* is

Education is the instilling and inculcation of *adab* in man — it is *ta'dīb*.[123] Thus *adab* is precisely what applies to man if he must acquit himself successfully and well in this life and the Hereafter. And the definition of education and its aims and purpose are already in fact contained in the brief exposition of the concept of *adab* as here outlined.

Islamic system of order and discipline
We referred earlier to an Islamic system of order and discipline. Islām itself is the epitome of the Divine cosmic order and discipline, and the man who is conscious of his destiny in Islām knows that in like manner he too is an order and discipline, in that he is like a city, a kingdom in miniature; for in him as in all mankind, is manifested the Attributes of the Creator without the reverse being the case. Man knows that he is knowing, and experience of such knowledge tells him that he is at once being and existence; a unity and yet a multiplicity, subsistent and at the same time evanescent — he is on the one hand *permanent*, and on the other *change*. His personality from his birth till his death as a phenomenal being remains unchanged, even though his physical being is everchanging and suffers final dissolution. And this is due to the fact that his personality refers to the permanent in him — his rational soul. Were it

---

transferred over to the state, there is danger that education becomes a secular exercise, which is happening in fact. Furthermore the end of *tarbiyah* is normally physical and material in character as it deals with physical and material growth only. Yet we all know that the real essence of the educational process is set towards the goal pertaining to the *intellect*, which inheres only in man. So we must select a precise term to denote education that fulfills the end and purpose of education, which is to produce a good man. The only appropriate and adequate term is *ta'dīb*. Error in the selection and application of terms employed for cultural, religious and spiritual concepts invariably leads to confusion in knowledge, in theory and in practice.

not for this quality of permanence, it would not be possible for knowledge to inhere in him. Thus the knowledge of the first kind, which is his life and food, refers to his rational soul; and his education as a whole and quest for knowledge leading to the first kind of knowledge, insofar as his personality is concerned, entails the pursuit of knowledge of the prerequisites to that first knowledge (*i. e.* the *farḍ'ayn*). In view of the permanent nature of his personality, so is education in Islām a continuous process throughout his life on earth, and it covers every aspect of that life. From the point of view of linguistic usage, we must see that the fact that the term *'ilm* has been applied in Islām to encompass the totality of life — the spiritual, intellectual, religious, cultural, individual and social — means that its character is universal, and that it is necessary to guide man to his salvation. No other culture and civilization has ever applied a single term for knowledge to encompass all activities in man's life. Perhaps this was why the organization, inculcation and dissemination of knowledge was conceived as a system of order and discipline pertaining to the *kulliyyah*, a concept conveying the idea of the *universal*. We know that from the earliest periods Islām began its educational system significantly with the mosque as its centre; and with the mosque (*jāmi'*) continuing to be its centre even — in some cases — till the present day, there developed other educational institutions such as the *maktab*; the *bayt al-ḥikmah*; the gatherings of scholars and students (*majālis*); the *dār al-'ulūm*, and the *madāris*; and in the fields of medicine, astronomy and devotional sciences there rose the hospitals, observatories, and *zāwiyah* within the Ṣūfī fraternities. We also know that the early Western universities were modelled after the Islamic originals. Very little information is available to me, however, concerning the original concept of the university within the Islamic system of education, and the extent to which original Islamic concepts pertaining to the structure of the university had influenced the Western copies. But the general character and structure of the universities today, which are veritable copies of Western models, still reveal significant traces of their Islamic origin.

The very name for the institution which derives from Latin: *universitatem* clearly reflects the original Islamic *kulliyyah.* Then again, apart from the role of medicine in Islamic learning and its early and great influence in the West, the anatomical concept of the *faculty,* which harks back on *quwwah* which refers to a *power inherent in the body of an organ,* is most significant, not only — it seems to me — in establishing its Islamic origin, but in demonstrating the fact that since the concept 'faculty' refers to a living being in whom the attribute 'knowledge' subsists, and that this knowledge is the governing principle determining his thought and action, the university must have been conceived in emulation of the general structure, in form, function and purpose, of *man.* It was meant to be a microcosmic representation of man — indeed, of the Universal Man (*al-insān al-kulliyy*).

But the university as it later was developed in the West and emulated today all over the world no longer reflects man. Like a man with no personality, the modern university has no abiding, vital *centre,* no permanent underlying principle establishing its final purpose. It still pretends to contemplate the universal and even claims to possess faculties and departments as if it were the body of an organ — but it has no brain, let alone intellect and soul, except only in terms of a purely administrative function of maintenance and physical development. Its dvelopment is not guided by a *final* principle and definite purpose, except by the relative principle urging on the pursuit of knowledge incessantly, with no absolute end in view. It is a symbol that has become ambiguous — unlike the Quranic concept of *āyah* — because it points to itself (*i. e.* to the sciences for the sake of the sciences) instead of to what it is meant to represent (*i. e.* to man), and hence is productive of perpetual confusion and even scepticism. Because of the secular basis of Western culture, which is mentioned in the beginning, the university is geared to a secular *relative* purpose, and hence reflects the secular *state* and *society* and not the universal man. But there never has been nor ever will be, *except in Islām in the person of the Holy Prophet,* upon whom be God's Blessings and Peace!, the Universal Man (*al-insān al-kāmil*) that can be reflected in microcosmic representation as 'university'. Neither can state nor society be truly considered as capable of possessing an attribute called knowledge, for that is only possessed by the individual man. And even if it be argued that the modern university is in fact emulating man, yet it is the *secular* man that is portrayed; the rational animal devoid of soul, like a circle with no centre. The various faculties and departments within them, like the various faculties and senses of the body, have in the modern university become uncoordinated, each preoccupied with its own endless pursuits; each exercising its own 'free will', as it were, and not the coherent will of one being, for there is no 'being' — all is 'becoming'. Can one be judged sane and coherent who contemplates some affair, and at the same time recognizes something else entirely different from what is being contemplated, and who says something again quite different altogether, who hears different sounds and sees yet again different things? The modern university is the epitome of man in a condition of *ẓulm,* and such a condition is maintained by the encouragement and elevation and legitimization of doubt and conjecture as epistemological tools of scientific enquiry. The Holy Qur'ān repeatedly repudiates such methods, branding them contraries of knowledge. Thus doubt (*shakk*), conjecture and guess (*ẓann*) disputation and contention (*mirā', i. q. jādala*), inclination of the mind or soul towards natural desire (*hawā*), are all generally considered blameworthy — the more so when applied to and masquerading as knowledge. We must take note of the significance that, in the case of Western culture and civilization, and with reference to the sociology of knowledge, the West has defined knowledge in terms of the effort of science as control of nature and society. With respect to man as an individual, to the improvement and identification and elevation of his personality and the desire to learn about the Divine order of the world and salvation, to this most important *purpose* — and hence true nature — of knowledge the West no longer attaches any significance and reality. This is and has been so by virtue of the fact that the West acknowledges no single Reality to fix its vision on; no single, valid Scripture to confirm and affirm in life; no single human Guide whose words and deeds and actions and entire mode of life can serve as model to emulate in life, as the Universal Man. We cannot, as Muslims, afford to overlook this important fact; for Islām embodies within itself all the three fundamentals of knowledge and action mentioned above, and for that reason alone classifies knowledge into two kinds and clarifies the concept of the knowledge of prerequisites (*farḍ'ayn*) that must form the basic core of all education. The following simple diagrams will help summarize in bare figurative framework the main subject of this chapter:

Fig. I:Man

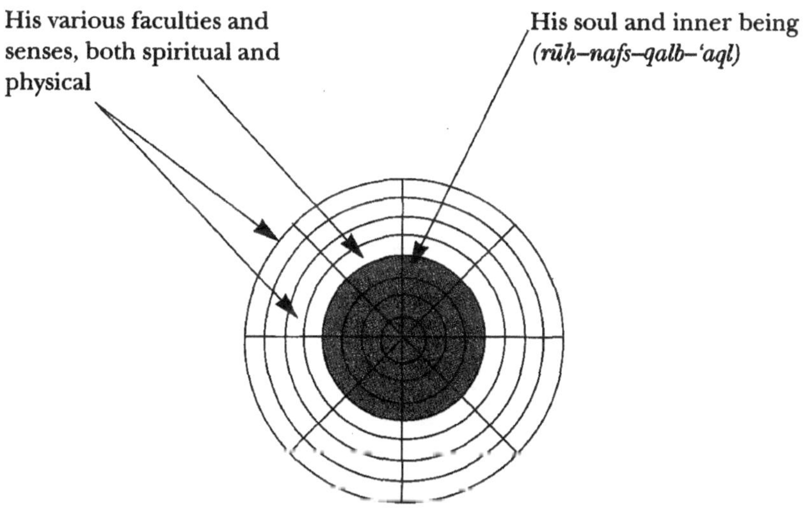

Knowledge of Sciences represents the *Farḍ Kifāyah* knowledge whose parts have been deployed according to priorities of service to self, state and society in the Muslim community)

Knowledge of Prerequisites to revealed knowledge (it represents the *Fard 'Ayn* knowledge) whose parts have been integrated to form the *core* knowledge for individuals in Islamic education.

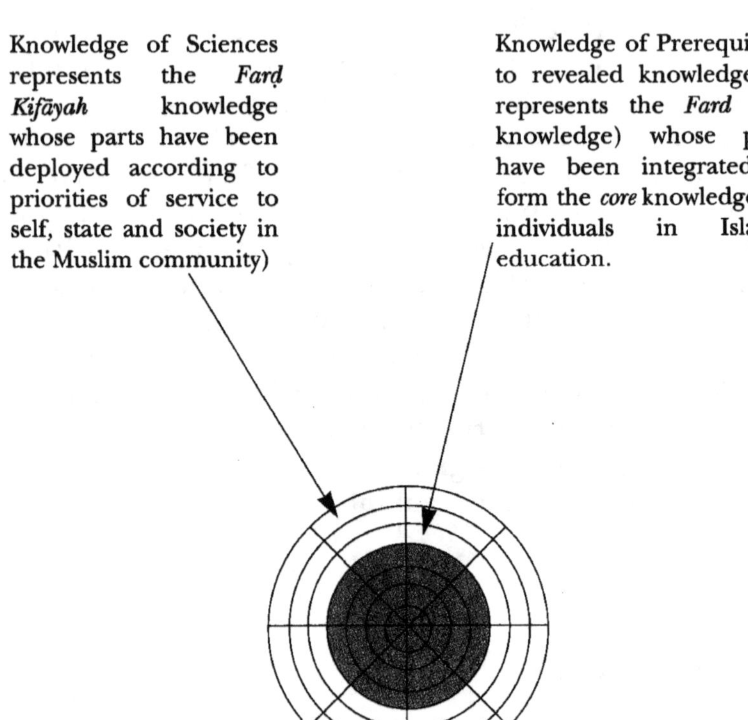

Fig. III: The Islamic University (as microcosmic
representation of the Universal Man in terms of knowledge

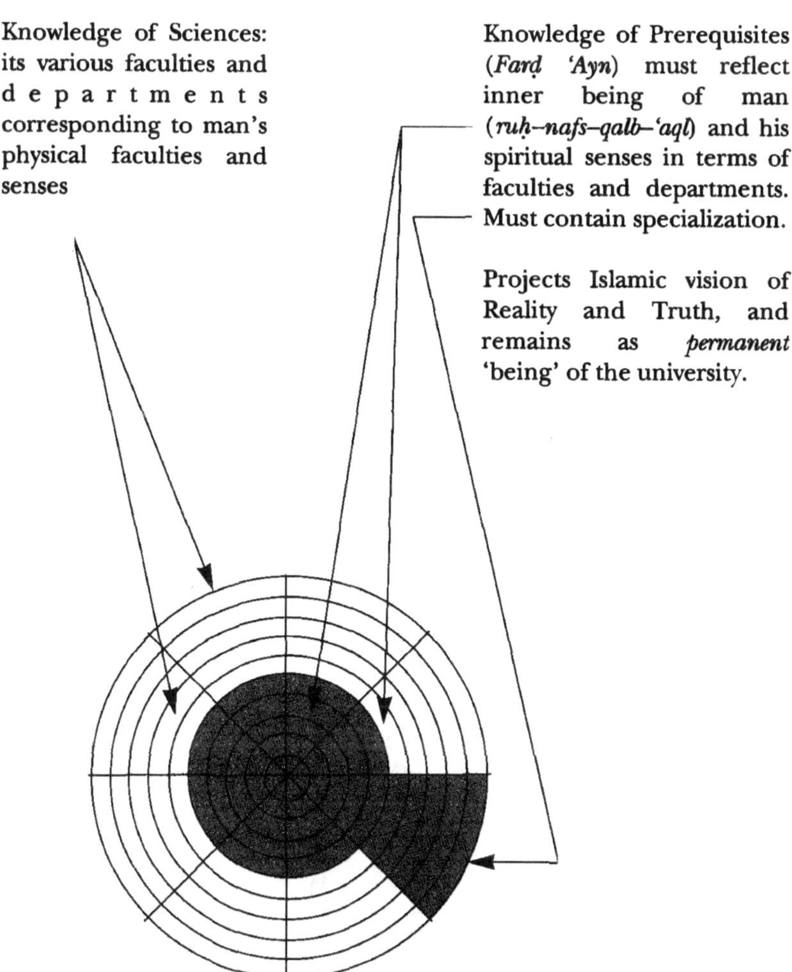

Knowledge of Sciences:
its various faculties and
d e p a r t m e n t s
corresponding to man's
physical faculties and
senses

Knowledge of Prerequisites
(*Farḍ 'Ayn*) must reflect
inner being of man
(*ruḥ–nafs–qalb–'aql*) and his
spiritual senses in terms of
faculties and departments.
Must contain specialization.

Projects Islamic vision of
Reality and Truth, and
remains as *permanent*
'being' of the university.

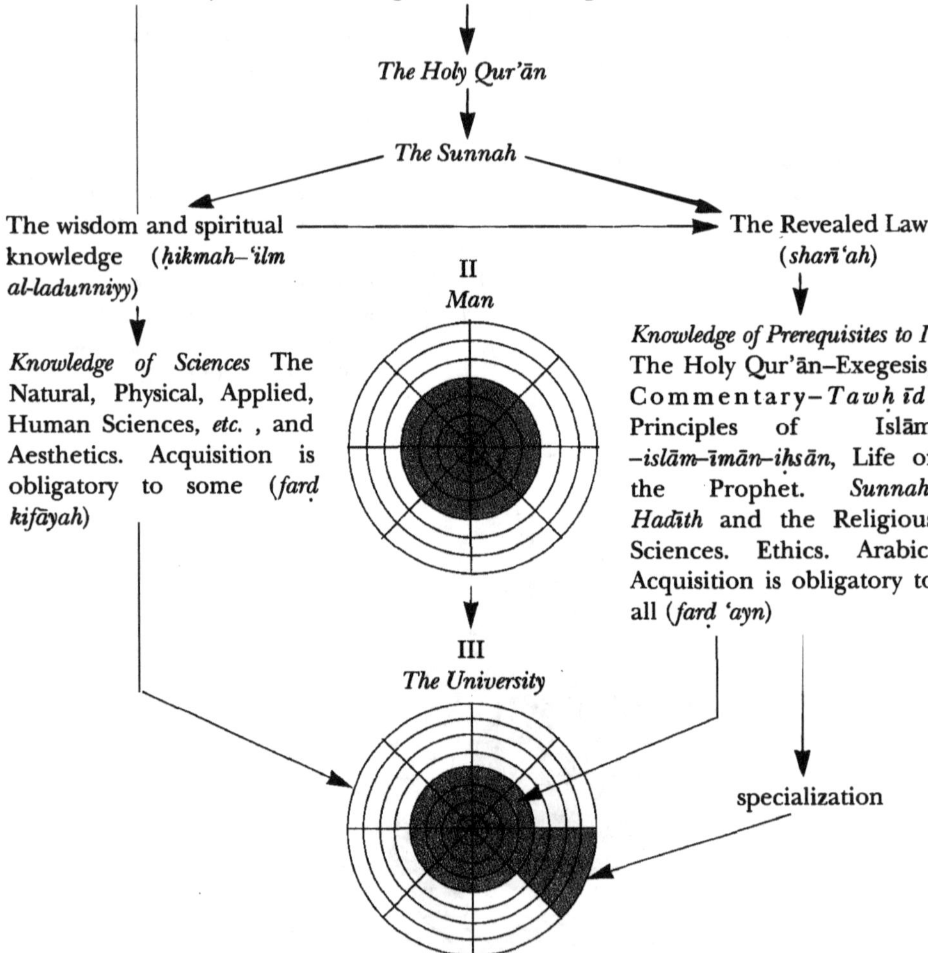

Note. With respect to the system of order and discipline sphere, the above Schema descends to the university, which is the highest level of the education system. However, the same pattern as outlined for the university applies to the lower levels in gradations from the lowest to the highest

Concluding Remarks and Suggestions

In the foregoing pages, including those of chapters II, III and IV of the book, I have attempted to elucidate certain *key concepts* pertaining to the nature and purpose of knowledge from the Islamic viewpoint, and to demonstrate the fundamental nature of their mutual interrelation and interdependence. These key concepts must form the essential elements of the Islamic system of education. They are:

1. The concept of religion (*dīn*);
2. The concept of man (*insān*);
3. The concept of knowledge (*'ilm* and *ma'rifah*);
4. The concept of wisdom (*ḥikmah*);
5. The concept of justice (*'adl*);
6. The concept of right action (*'amal* as *adab*);
7. The concept of the university (*kulliyyah-jāmi'ah*);

In terms of practical application, the first refers to the *purpose* of seeking knowledge and involvement in the process of education; the second to the *scope*; the third to the *content*; the fourth to the *criteria* in relation to the second and the third; the fifth to the *deployment* in relation to the fourth; the sixth to the *method* in relation to the first down to the fifth; and the seventh to the *form of implementation* in relation to all that precedes it.

In elucidating the key concepts pertaining to the nature and purpose of knowledge, and in demonstrating the fundamental nature of their mutual interrelation and interdependence, we have in this and the previous chapters touched briefly but significantly upon the origin, structure, methods and validity of knowledge in the context of Islām. Indeed, the problem of knowledge is the recurrent theme of this book, and although we stated in a previous note that in this chapter we are concerned not so much with a philosophical or epistemological definition of knowledge, but more with its general classification designed to be applied to a system of order and discipline that describes the Islamic educational system, it nevertheless is important to understand what the Islamic epistemological context involves and implies. Since we have said that all knowledge comes from God and is interpreted by the soul through its spiritual and physical faculties, it follows that the most suitable epistemological definition would be that knowledge, with reference to God as being its origin, is the arrival *(ḥuṣūl)* in the soul of the meaning *(ma'nā)* of a thing or an object of knowledge; and that with reference to the soul as being its interpreter, knowledge is the arrival *(wuṣūl)* of the soul at the meaning of a thing or an object of knowledge. The World of Nature, as depicted in the Holy Qur'ān, is like a Great Book; and every detail therein, encompassing the farthest horizons and our very selves, is like a word in that Great Book that speaks to man about its Author. The word as it really is is a sign, a symbol; and to know it as it really is is to know what it stands for, what it symbolizes, what it means. To study the word as word, regarding it as if it had an independent reality of its own, is to miss the real point of studying it, for regarded as such it is no longer a sign or a symbol, as it is being made to point to itself, which is not what it really is. So in like manner, the study of Nature, of any thing, any object of knowledge in Creation, pursued in order to attain knowledge of it; if the expression 'as it really is' is taken to mean its alleged independent reality, essentially and existentially, or its perseity, as if it were something ultimate and self-subsistent — then such study is devoid of real purpose, and the pursuit of knowledge becomes a deviation from the truth, which necessarily puts into question the validity of such knowledge. For as it really is, a thing or an object of knowledge is other than what it is, and that 'other' — at least at the rational and empirical level of normal experience — refers to its meaning. This is why we have defined knowledge epistemologically as the arrival in the soul of the *meaning* of a thing, or the arrival by the soul at the *meaning* of a thing. When we speak of 'rational' and 'empirical' as we do here, we are not thereby subscribing to the principal cleavage along methodological lines determined by what is called rationalism on the one hand, and empiricism on the other, as here we are deliberating in an Islamic context which is not the same as that of Western philosophy and epistemology. Reason and experience are in Islām valid channels by which knowledge is attained — knowledge, that is, at the rational and empirical level of normal experience. We maintain that there is another level; but even at this other, spiritual level, reason and experience are still valid, only that they are of a transcendental order. At this level the rational has merged with the intellectual, the empirical with what pertains to authentic spiritual experiences such as inner witnessing (*shuhūd*), tasting (*dhawq*) and other interrelated states of trans-empirical awareness. This is the level at which *taṣawwuf*, which I have defined earlier as 'the practice of the *sharī'ah* at the station (*maqām*) of *iḥsān*', becomes the context in which knowledge means unification (*tawḥīd*).

In appraising the present situation with regard to the formulation and dissemination of knowledge in the Muslim world, we must see that infiltration of key concepts from the Western world has brought confusion which will ultimately cause grave consequences if left unchecked. Since what is formulated and disseminated in and through universities and other institutions of learning from the lower to the higher levels is in fact knowledge *infused* with the character and personality of Western culture and civilization and *moulded* in the crucible of Western culture (see *Introduction*), our task will be first to *isolate the elements* including the key concepts which make up that culture and civilization (see the last paragraph in pp. 137 - 138 above). These elements and key concepts are mainly prevalent in that branch of knowledge pertaining to the human sciences, although it must be noted that even in the natural, physical and applied sciences, particularly where they deal with *interpretation of facts* and *formulation of theories*, the same process of isolation of the elements and key concepts should be applied, for the interpretations and formulations indeed belong to the sphere of the human sciences. The 'islamization' of present-day knowledge means precisely that, *after* the isolation process referrred to, the knowledge free of the elements and key concepts isolated are *then* infused with the Islamic elements and key concepts which, in view of their fundamental nature as defining the *fiṭrah*, in fact imbue the knowledge with the quality of its natural function and purpose and thus makes it *true knowledge*.[124] It will not do to accept present-day knowledge as it is, and then hope to 'islamize' it merely by 'grafting' or 'transplanting' into it Islamic sciences and principles; this method will but produce conflicting results not altogether beneficial nor desirable. Neither 'grafting' nor 'transplant' can produce the desired result when the 'body' is already possessed by foreign elements and consumed in disease. The foreign elements and disease will have first to be drawn out and neutralized before the body of knowledge can be remoulded in the crucible of Islām.

Our next important task will be the formulation and integration of the essential Islamic elements and key concepts so as to produce a composition which will comprise the core knowledge to be deployed in our educational system from the lower to the higher levels in respective gradations designed to conform to the standard of each level. The core knowledge at the university level, which must first be formulated before that at any other level, must be composed of ingredients pertaining to the nature of man (*insān*); the nature of religion (*dīn*) and man's involvement in it; of knowledge (*'ilm* and *ma'rifah*), wisdom (*ḥikmah*) and justice (*'adl*) with respect to man and his religion; the nature of right action (*'amal-adab*). These will have to be referred to the concept of God, His Essence and Attributes (*tawḥīd*); the Revelation (the Holy Qur'ān), its meaning and message; the Revealed Law (*sharī'ah*) and what necessarily follows: the Prophet (upon whom be God's Bessings and Peace!), his life and *sunnah*, and the history and message of the Prophets before him. They will also

---

124 True knowledge conforms with *fiṭrah.* The sentence answers the argument posed in p. 138 above. See also note 116.

have to be referred to knowledge of the Principles and practice of Islām, the religious sciences (*'ulūm al-shar'iyyah*), which must include legitimate elements of *taṣawwuf* and Islamic philosophy, including valid cosmological doctrines pertaining to the hierarchy of being, and knowledge of Islamic ethics and moral principles and *adab*. To this must be added knowledge of the Arabic language and of the Islamic worldview as a whole. This core knowledge, integrated and composed as a harmonious unity and designed at the university level as a model structure and content for the other levels, must invariably be reflected in successively simpler forms at the secondary and primary levels of the educational system. At each level, the core knowledge must be designed to be made identical for application in the educational system throughout the Muslim world, since the core knowledge is obligatory ot *all* Muslims (*farḍ'ayn*).

With respect to the knowledge of the sciences designated as obligatory to some only (*farḍ kifāyah*), it has been pointed out that it must be imbued with the Islamic elements and key concepts *after* the foreign elements and key concepts have been isolated from its every branch. To this knowledge must be added the knowledge of Islamic history, culture and civilization, Islamic thought, and the development of the sciences in Islām. In this category too new courses on comparative religion from the Islamic point of view, on Western culture and civilization, must be designed as a means for Muslims to understand the culture and civilization that has been and is and will continue to be confronting Islām. Knowledge of all these will assure logical continuity in the successive educational progression from the core knowledge to that of the sciences. Many new subjects will undoubtedly be added to the above. The determining of the order of priority, with reference to individual striving after the various branches of the knowledge of the sciences, will invariably depend on its relative usefulness and benefit to self, society, and state respectively. The formulation of the concept of 'relative usefulness and benefit to self, society and state' must be contained in the form of general principles reflecting the Islamic elements and key concepts. It follows that the order of priority with reference to choice must not be left to the judgement of inviduals, but must likewise be planned to conform with the current needs of self-society-state, which is none other than those of the Community. Whereas in the case of the core knowledge the obligation to acquire it is directed to all and to both sexes, in the case of knowledge of the sciences, certain branches may not be deemed appropriate for women; so that some may be obligtatory to men only and some to women. Regarding entrance into the higher levels of education, it is not sufficient merely for an individual to be allowed to qualify on the basis of good results in formal scientific subjects, as is practised today everywhere. No doubt personal conduct is recognized as important in many educational systems, but their notions of personal conduct are vague and not really applied effectively in education, and no objective system has been devised to determine the nature of those elements of human conduct and behaviour that are undesirable for purposes of higher learning leading to appointments to responsible posts and offices. It is neither impossible nor impracticable to devise a system for implementation into the educational framework whereby certain individuals can be barred from higher education. Knowledge (*i. e.* the *farḍ kifāyah*) is not necessarily everyone's right; no one in Islām has the right to do wrong — this would be a contradiction in terms and purpose. To do wrong is injustice, and this is not a *right.* The doing something wrong that is considered in Islām to be the most destructive to self, society, and state revolves around three vices: lying, breaking promise, and betraying trust. The Holy Qur'ān is most emphatic in denouncing these vices as they are vices which caused man's downfall and which man not only perpetrates on his fellowman, but even on God Himself! Hence the profound significance of the *ḥadīth* narrated by Abū Hurayrah, may God be well pleased with him!, concerning the mark of the hypocrite, that when he speaks, he lies; and when he promises, he breaks the promise; and when he is entrusted with something he betrays the trust

اذاحدث كذب واذا وعد خلف واذا ائتمن خان

I say that this well-known *ḥadīth* is of profound significance not only because it states in succinct summary the precise nature of the most destructive of man's vices, but also because it furnishes us with clear indication of the *criteria* to be adopted when judging human character and conduct. I believe that the *ḥadīth* is not meant to be heeded simply as wise counsel whose application is to be left to individual judgement and responsibility, but that it must be seriously systematized into an educational devise which can be applied as a moral check on all who will pass through the educational process. Such a devise, applied positively and effectively through the levels of the educational system, will assist in minimizing the emergence and perpetration in Muslim society and state and leaderhsip of betrayal of trust leading to injustice and ignorance.

Space does not permit us to go into details here. This chapter is meant to set forth a statement of the problem and the possible and acceptable solution to it; to gather together the key concepts and explain them in the correct Islamic persepctive. If at all this humble attempt to meet the demands of this task in any small way contributes to the true and the correct answer, then to God alone the Praise, for every atom of good is accomplished through His help and guidance.

The details of the formulation and integration of the core knowledge, the order of deployment of the knowledge of the sciences in the academic structure and in the priority framework in the system of order and discipline, will have to be methodically set forth after thorough research by a team of expert scholars and thinkers experienced in academic administration. This team should be gathered together in one place where recourse to the necessary facilities can conveniently be had, and where consultations, discussions and research among the members can be facilitated and coordinated without undue expenditure in the human and financial resources and in time. The blueprint for the above proposed concept and for the restructuring of the academic and administrative system according to priorities can then be prepared in a few years. When this is accomplished, the experimental stage, beginning with the university, can commence operations. Naturally, the assistance and support of the wise and far-sighted Muslim government desirous of achieving the results of this long-term but realistic project is urgently sought, both at the initial stage of reserach and preparation of the blueprint, and at the experimental stage of setting up the Islamic university. This might take several years of critical assessment and appraisal of the functioning of its implementation according to plan, and will involve evaluation of at least the first intake of graduates; of methodical analysis and correction of errors in the process of perfecting the system until it is found to be satisfactory. When this stage has been achieved, the system can then be recommended to the Muslim world at large, and the follow-up in connection with the lower levels of the educational system can be planned and implemented after the pattern of the university has been perfected. It is futile to attempt short-term myopic measures in providing for a solution to a problem of this magnitude. Our great and God-fearing pre-decessors of astute vision and profound intellectual and spiritual depth have laboured in terms of centuries to build splendid systems of thought and action with God's help and guidance, and if we are even to hope to rise to the same expectation, then we must humbly emulate their example.

Appendix

ON ISLAMIZATION: THE CASE OF THE MALAY-INDONESIAN ARCHIPELAGO

About ten years ago*, writing on the historical and cultural impact of Islām upon the Malay world which revolutionized the Malay vision of reality and existence into a distinctly Islamic world view, I referred to the process that brought about this phenomenon as *islamization*, the integral components of which form part of the dimensions of Islām. I wrote then (S.M.N. al-Attas, *Preliminary Statement on a General Theory of the Islamization of the Malay-Indonesian Archipelago*, Kuala Lumpur, 1969), that

> ...the coming of Islām seen from the perspective of modern times [that is, seen from the perspective of our present time when we can 'look back' into the effects of historical processes which are found to have radically changed the lives and worlds of men, and discern their causes and specific and general influences], was the most momentous event in the history of the Archi-pelago.(p.2).

In this connection I also drew attention to the

> ...similarities that exist between the dominant role of Islām in influencing the beginnings of the European Middle Ages as Pirenne pointed out [H. Pirenne, *Mohammed and Charlemagne*, London, 1958], and the

---

I.e in 1967.

role of Islām in transforming, so to speak, both the soul
and the body of the Malay-Indonesian society. (p.7).
As a historical and cultural process islamization in the
Archipelago underwent three phases.

Phase I: from approximately 578-805/1200-1400, jurisprudence or *fiqh* played the major role of interpreting
the religious law (*sharī'ah*) in the conversion of the
Malays. The conversion was effected by strength of
faith, not necessarily accompanied by an understanding of the rational and intellectual implications such
conversion entailed. Fundamental concepts connected
with the central Islamic concept of Unity of God
(*tawḥīd*) were still vague in the minds of the converts,
their old concepts overlapping and clouding or confusing the new ones. This phase can well be described
as the conversion of the 'body'.

Phase II: from approximately 803-1112/1400-1700, continuation of the process described in Phase I, but
during this phase the major role of interpreting the
religious law had passed on to philosophical mysticism
and metaphysics (*taṣawwuf*) and other rational and
intellectual elements such as rational theology (*kalām*).
During this phase, Ṣūfism and Ṣūfi writings primarily
and the writings of the Mutakallimūn played the
dominant role aimed at the conversion of the 'spirit'.
Fundamental concepts introduced according to the
Islamic *weltanschauung*, some of which were still
understood in the opaque sense, influenced by the old
weltanschauung, were expounded and defined so that
they were understood in both the transparent and
semi-transparent senses.

Phase III: from approximately 1112/1700 onwards,
continuation of Phase I and consummation of Phase II
which had been largely successful. To this phase must
also be assigned the cultural influences brought about
by the coming of the West. What is generally known as
"Westernization" is here conceived as the perpetuation
of the rationalistic, individualistic, and international-

istic spirit whose philosophical foundations were laid earlier by Islām. (pp. 29-30).

As a background to the evaluation of the major changes in the world view of the peoples of the Archipelago which were brought about by the coming of Islām, an outline survey of the philosophical and religious situation in the Archipelago before the coming of Islām was focussed towards the relevant perspective.

Hinduism, as the people of the Archipelago practised it, was a superstructure maintained by the ruling group above an indifferent community. The community's participation in Hinduism was a necessary influence from above; the religion was imposed on the community by the authority of the ruling group. The Malay-Indonesian society was therefore not a Hinduized society, rather the Malay-Indonesian dynasties were, to use the expression of Van Leur, "legitimized sacrally by an Indian hierocracy" [J.C. Van Leur, *Indonesian Trade and Society*, The Hague, 1955, p. 108]. The philosophical influence of Hinduism upon the Malay-Indonesian world view has been unduly magnified [by the Dutch and British orientalists]. The people of the Archipelago were more aesthetic than philosophical by nature; they either did not fully grasp the subtleties of Hindu metaphysics or they ignored it in favour of that which was less complicated and more readily acceptable to their own worldview. Philosophy was transformed into art at the expense of the rational and intellectual elements. Intellectual speculation, with its emphasis on logic and systematic reasoning, did not seem to have been popular. No doubt the doctrine of the *Ātman* as propounded in the *Bhagavad Gītā* was known and made to run through the veins of Hindu-Malay literature to give to it some life-giving spark of the divine. But we must not be misled into thinking that there was anything really profound in the sense in which it is propounded in the Hindu doctrines. The doctrine of the *Ātman* interpreted as the *Brahman* 'lodged within' the individual being was congenial to the autochthonous world view of the Hindu-Malay which was still steeped in animism... [Hindu-Malay literature was mainly mythological and presented] in poetic form lacking exposition and commentary so that it was not meant for the profane ears of the masses. For this latter group, the philosophical world view envisioned by the poets of Old Javanese literature was glimpsed in the *wayangs* [plays for the various kinds of theatre or theatrical dancing] filtered, as it were, through the medium of art.

The same could also be said of Buddhism in the Archipelago. For many centuries, from the /6th to the 5th/IIth centuries, Sumatra seems to have been a great centre of Buddhism and Buddhist philosophy. Yet the influence of the Buddhist clergy in Sumatra did not seem to have made itself felt in the realm of philosophy, but again in that of art. It is further significant that this artistic manifestation occurred in Java in the form of the great Borobudur. We are told of the existence of one thousand monks in Sumatra in the late 6th century where Buddhist theology and philosophy flourished; of the venerable Atisha, the great reformer of Buddhism in Tibet, who had sat at the feet of Dharmakirti, high priest of the Buddhist clergy in Sumatra in the early 5th/IIth century. Considering the powerful influence of the Sumatran Buddhist clergy in producing reformers in different lands, it is strange and surprising that Buddhist philosophy did not flourish as well in Sumatra itself. It is possible that Buddhism, not being a missionary religion charged with an expansive movement, was not interested in imparting a new worldview to the people of the Archipelago. It may also be possible that the Buddhist clergy in Sumatra was mainly not composed of indigenous people but of people from South India who came there to find seclusion and peace for the purpose of contemplation, who ... shut themselves up in their monasteries oblivious of the outside world. Neither the Hindu-Malay nor the Buddhist-Malay, as far as we know, had produced any thinker or philosopher of note... (pp. 2-4).

Islām came to the Archipelago couched in Ṣūfi metaphysics. It was through *taṣawwuf* that the highly intellectual and rationalistic religious spirit entered the receptive minds of the people, effecting a rise of rationalism and intellectualism not manifested in pre-Islamic times. This emergence of rationalism and intellectualism can be viewed as the powerful spirit that set in motion the process of revolutionizing the Malay-Indonesian worldview, turning it away from a crumbling world of mythology, which can be compared with the Greek world in the Olympian era, to the world of intelligence, reason and order. The disseminators of Islām propagated the belief in a God Whose Power is governed by His Wisdom; Whose Creative Will acts in accordance with Reason. Man is conceived as the epitome of Creation; that in the ring of universal life, Man is the superscription and the seal. The essence of Man is that he is rational and rationality is the connection between him and Reality. It is these concepts and that of the spiritual equality between man and man that gave the ordinary man a sense of worth and nobility denied him in pre-Islamic times...(pp. 5-6).

The result of a preliminary semantic study of the key cultural terms connected with concepts of God, Being, Existence, Time, Religion, Man, the Self and Will reveal the great changes that have occurred in the Malay-Indonesian worldview caused by Islamic elements. The animistic elements in the old worldview coupled with its logical notion of a Parmenidean universe with all its implications have been supplanted by rationalistic elements involving an atomistic, dynamic universe. The concept of the Self is now highly abstract. The Self does not belong to the spatio-temporal order, and this in turn influences the concepts of Will and its relation to freedom and morality. The connotations in the old feudal concepts were replaced by new and different ones. New culture values replaced the old. (pp. 7-8).

...While Hinduism and Buddhism...might not have had much effect in changing the essential character and world view of the Malay-Javanese civilization, the same view cannot be applied with regard to Islām. The differences between the spirit of the former religion and that of Islām, their places of origin, their religious mediums, their initial and significant influences — on the Javanese civilization in the case of the former, and the Malay in the case of the latter — are so considerable that to entertain such a view would be highly fallacious ...Hinduism is not a Semitic religion based upon an uncompromising monotheism charged with a missionary spirit. It is true that the metaphysical formulations of Semitic monotheism become almost identical with those of Hinduism at certain levels, yet they are generally conceived by their respective adherents as considerably dissimilar. The several formulations of Hinduism — even in its country of origin — have been preponderantly of an aesthetic nature... The scientific formulations of the metaphysical doctrines of the religion cannot be said to be generally recognized and accepted. By nature the Javanese civilization was more aesthetic than scientific. The scientific part of Hindu philosophy and metaphysics was ignored in favour of what was more congenial to the autochthonous world view. It was aesthetic and ritualistic Hinduism that was recognized and accepted; the scientific, with its emphasis on the rational and intellectual elements and on systematic and logical analysis, was rejected — and even when accepted had first to be sifted through the sieve of art so that the worldview presented was that envisioned by poets rather than by thinkers and philosophers. Hinduism is couched in symbolic forms that are aesthetic and anthropomorphic, no doubt in large measure due to the influence of the language which forms its medium of expression. The same conclusions may be drawn with respect to the Old Javanese language. There has been, furthermore, a preference for poetry rather than for prose in the languages of the two civilizations, Indian and Javanese ...The essential religious spirit of Islām is monotheistic, couched in its unique conception of the Unity of God (*al-tawḥīd*). Conceived philosophically through rational theology and metaphysics (*'ilm al-kalām* and *taṣawwuf*), it sets forth an ontology, cosmology and psychology of its own in its conception of the Oneness of Being (*waḥdat al-wujūd*). This ontology, cosmology and psychology is not to be equated simply with that of Neo-Platonism and Hinduism according to the *Vedanta*, as it in general has its foundations in the *Qur'ān* whose uniqueness has impressed itself upon every facet of Muslim life. The Qur'ān came together with Islām to the Malay-Indonesian Archipelago. No comparable event occurred in pre-Islamic times to match that of the impact and influence of the Qur'ān, as no complete Holy Scripture ever seems to have existed in the past. The Qur'anic conception of man as a rational animal, capable by means of his reason or intelligence (*'aql*) of understanding and appreciating the signs (*āyāt*) that point to God is made all the more significant in respect of the future development of the Malay language by the emphasis laid on the meaning of 'rational' (*nāṭiq*) as the capacity to speak (*berkata-kata* [*i.e.,* speaking]) — the emphasis on the faculty of speech. Now it is not just the capacity to speak that is being emphasized as the rationality in man but more significant, the capacity to speak clearly; to employ correct and unambiguous symbols and signs in interpreting experience and reality. Indeed, perhaps no other Holy Book has so impressed upon man the importance and uniqueness of language. The Qur'ān alone claims clarity (*mubīn*) as being one of its most important chief virtues. It had chosen Arabic to be its language because of the inherent scientific tendency towards clarity in the structure of Arabic [Pre-Islamic Arabic, not being an aesthetic religious language, whose vocabulary is generally enriched or emburdened as the case may be by the sophisticated and inevitably confusing mythological, mystical, metaphysical and philosophical vocabularies, was comparatively 'pure' and unsophisticated, as far as the purpose of Islām was concerned, in relation to the Graeco-Roman and Irano-Persian languages that held sway in the neighbouring regions (p. 23)]. The preference is for prose rather than for poetry (*shi'r*), and even when poetry is used later in religious and metaphysical topics its excellence is not considered merely from the point of view of the science of prosody but, more important, from that of exposition of meaning, interpretation, and commentary achieved through *sharḥ* (lit. from the root "to open" or "to interpret the true meaning"). A whole science of Islamic prosody is evolved out of the Qur'ān; it is also the sole authority on Arabic and its grammar. Arabic is the language of Islām and no language of any Muslim people, whether or not it has achieved a lofty rank in civilization, is without the influence of Arabic. The Qur'ān also inaugurated among the Arabs themselves the tradition of a written language, and wherever oral tradition was the literary tradition of a people, it was the influence of the Qur'ān that, having effected conversion to Islām, brought about the transition to a written literary tradition. All the Muslim peoples adopted the Arabic script, creating wherever necessary new letters to represent the phonetic peculiarities not found in Arabic but still basing such letters on the Arabic script... Islamic [culture] as opposed to Hinduism and Buddhism, is a scientific and literary culture. (pp. 19-21).

The Qur'an, when it came upon the Arabs, extolling clarity and intelligence, declares itself to be in "plain" (*kitābun fuṣṣilat āyātuhu*) and "not devious" (*ghayra dhī 'iwajin*) Arabic. By relative comparison, as far as aesthetic religion was concerned, the relationship between Arabic on the one hand and the Graeco-Roman and Irano-Persian languages on the other, was like Malay and Old Javanese, the latter being the dominant aesthetic literary and religious language of the Archipelago. Semantically, Old Javanese would have been less susceptible than Malay of recognizing and accepting the Quranic teachings, since its understanding of them would have been more clouded or confused by the existing and firmly rooted concepts and ideas in its aesthetic religious vocabulary. (pp. 23-24).

...The Malay language underwent a revolutionary change; apart from enrichment of a great part of its vocabulary by a large number of Arabic and Persian words, it became the chief medium for conveying Islām throughout the Archipelago so that by the 9th/16th century, at the latest, it had achieved the status of a literary and religious language displacing the hegemony of Javanese...Malay literature flourished — and there are reasons to believe that it even originated — in the Islamic period. The 9th/16th and 10th/17th centuries witnessed the unrivalled prolificness of Malay writing on philosophical mysticism and rational theology. The first Malay translation of the Qur'ān with commentary based on al-Bayḍāwī's famous Commentary, and translations, commentaries and original works on philosophical mysticism and rational theology also appeared during this period which marked the rise of rationalism and intellectualism not manifested anywhere before in the Archipelago. Corresponding to what I have outlined as Phase II of the islamization process, this period was significant in setting in motion the process of revolutionizing the Malay-Indonesian *weltanschauung* effecting its transformation from an aesthetic to a scientific one. The underlying factor in this cultural revolution was the clarification of a new conception of Being introduced by Islām. It is the correct comprehension of this new conception of Being that constituted the inner intensification of the islamization process. The Malay language, it seems to me, developed into a new stream as a result of its being employed as the vehicle for philosophical discourse in the Archipelago. This new stream, probably originating in Barus, had its centre in Pasai (later Acheh), the earliest centre of Islamic learning in the Archipelago, whence its influence spread throughout the Archi-pelago. The new stream is characterized by its terse, clear style, its Islamic vocabulary; it reveals a language of logical reasoning and scientific analysis very much influenced no doubt by its writers — Ṣufīs, scholars, translators, and commentators — who were themselves under the sway of the Qur'ān which, as I have already pointed out, extolls clarity and intelligence in speech and writing. It is from this new stream that 'modern' Malay or the present day Malay-Indonesian language developed, since this was the stream that conveyed and spread Islām in the Archipelago...To this same period must modern Malay historical writing be assigned. (pp. 27-29).

...So widely was the language spread by Islām that it is now the official language of over 100 million people, perhaps the second largest Muslim language. (p. 27)... Together with the historical factor, the religious and language factors began setting in motion the process towards a national consciousness. It is the logical conclusion of this process that created the evolution of the greater part of the Archipelago into the modern Indonesian nation with Malay as its national language. (p. 8).

...The coming of Islām constituted the inauguration of a new period in the history of the Malay-Indonesian Archipelago. The greatest evidence of this cultural revolution manifested itself in expository and polemical writings during the 8th/15th to the 10th/17th centuries reflecting the change of ideas in the worldview of the people centered around a different conception of Being from what they had known in the past. This was also the 'clarification', 'intensification' and 'standardization' of Islām followed by 'correction', to complete the change, as it were. Ṣūfi metaphysics did not come, contrary to what is held even by some Muslim scholars, to harmonize Islām with traditional beliefs grounded in Hindu-Buddhist beliefs and other autochthonous traditions; it came to *clarify the difference* between Islām and what they had known in the past. Indeed, the whole period, from the testimony of the writings, was devoted to answering the ever increasingly persistent question and demand for clarification of the nature of Being. The fact that the question was raised at all revealed the existence of an inner problem experienced by the Malay-Indonesian. No such polemics or raising of such questions were ever known to have occurred before, as no such problem was encountered at the coming of Hinduism and Buddhism. Major key terms represented by Malay words having to do with God, Man and the relationship between them and the World, underwent examination, distinction and acceptance or rejection in relation to Arabic key terms and words philosophically analogous to what happened to Arabic itself during the Translation Period when it became the vehicle of Greek philosophy and was influenced by Greek thought.

The spiritual revolution manifested in the 8th/15th-10th/17th centuries reflected the beginnings of the modern age in the Archipelago. The concept modern has nowhere, to my mind, been clarified when scholars apply it in the context of the Malay-Indonesian Archipelago or, for that matter, of the Muslims as a whole. (p. 30).

...Religion in Western culture has always been conveyed through the medium of art. Rational theology and philosophical speculations on God were initiated later after greater acquaintance with Greek philosophy became possible through the paradoxically significant contact with Islām. Even then, religion remained in the firm embrace of art, as it does now. Philosophy and science divorced themselves from religion, though not from art, disenchanted from its lack of certainty. The introduction of Christianity to Europe, just as that of Hinduism and Buddhism to the Archipelago, has never been followed by a rationalistic clarification of the conception of Being. This task, as far as Christianity was concerned, was left to philosophy which reduced religion to a mere theory, and even then it occurred in comparatively recent times. Indeed, it can be said, perhaps without exaggeration, that the very nature of the problem which lay within the inmost ground of Western culture has its roots in the frustrations in early Christian theological polemics and disputes which in turn gave rise to all manner of "developments" in philosophy, in science, in humanism, and in what is considered today as "modern".(pp. 22-23).

...In Europe itself in the cultural history of the Western Christian peoples, the concept "modern" is traced back to the rationalistic, individualistic and internationalistic spirit which began to emerge in the 7th/14th century onwards. But, again, what constitutes what is modern is very much dependent upon the religion. In Western Christian cultural history, it was the very religion, as interpreted by the Church, that gave rise to the attitude conceived as modern so that the very meaning of the term is governed by Christian doctrine which ultimately rest with the clergy...it was conflict with and opposition to the teachings of the Church that brought about the modern attitude, that is, rationalism, individualism and internationalism which in the West has always been understood as humanism. Clearly, such a concept cannot be applied to Muslims, for in Islām there has always been neither 'Church' in the Western

Christian sense nor clergy, and the rationalism, indivi
dualism and internationalism understood by the
Muslim has always been in harmony, not conflict, with
religion. The above statements have profound implications embracing the distinct philosophical and religious attitudes of Islām and the West (Christianity).
(pp. 30-31).

Some of these "profound implications embracing the distinct philosophical and religious attitudes of Islām and the
West (Christianity)" are outlined in the present book. With
reference to Phase III of the process of islamization quoted
above (Appendix, p. 170) in which I stated that "what is
generally known as "Westernization"is here conceived as
the perpetuation of the rationalistic, individualistic and
internationalistic spirit whose philosophical foundations
were laid earlier by Islam", I said that

...In the Archipelago, the coming of Western imperialism as well as the imposition of Western culture
beginning in the 10th/16th century certainly seem to
have interrupted and retarded the process of islamization. Before this period, there were other forces
operating in the Islamic world as a whole such as
internal political dissensions and the decline in
political and economic power. Furthermore, advancement in the field of the technological sciences in
Europe, coupled with the lack of such advancement in
the Islamic world, weakened the latter considerably.
These disastrous events occurring in the Islamic world
caused reprecussions in the Archipelago. But the
appearance of Europeans on the Malay-Indonesian
scene and their control over the area beginning from
the 11th/17th century to the present century have left
their effects upon the Muslims. In certain parts of the
Archipelago, Western influences have resurrected the
pre-Islamic feudal order; in modern times we witness
the revivification of feudal tendencies: old customs
devoid of coherent culture values, old titles, court tradi
tions, *etc.* Western scholars engaged in Malay-

Indonesian history have neglected and minimized the importance of the study of Islām and its role in the Archipelago. Prejudice against and fear of Islām have influenced Western imperialism in attempting a consistent policy of separating Muslims from their religion, as has been the case with the Dutch and British powers in the Archipelago. This was generally effected by the control of religious administration, and thereby the religion itself, through the local ruling groups. At the same time, the system of education has neglected the teaching of Islām. (p. 9).

...On the other hand, however, the coming of the West, seen solely from the perspective of a cultural phenomenon and not an imperialistic one, can be considered as a continuation of the islamization process; it can be considered to have perpetuated the rationalistic spirit, the philosophical foundations of which had already been laid by Islām long before. It is when seen in this perspective that, to use a pregnant remark, Islām had prepared the Archipelago, in a sense, for the modern world to come.(pp. 9-10).

Earlier in the present book (p. 44) I defined islamization as the liberation of man first from magical, mythological, animistic, national-cultural tradition opposed to Islām, and then from secular control over his reason and his language. The man of Islām is he whose reason and language are no longer controlled by magic, myth, superstition, animism, his own cultural and national traditions opposed to Islām and secularism. What I meant when I referred to westernization seen solely from the perspective of a cultural phenomenon as being a continuation of the islamization process referred in fact to the general effect westernization had in the disintegration of the magical world view of the Malay-Indonesian. Islām had already initiated the process of that disintegration, and westernization continued that process, which is not completely accomplished yet. On the other hand westernization revived the non-Islamic cultural and national traditions opposed to Islām and set an educational, administrative and political course heading towards secular 'development'. It is only the perpetuation of the 'rationalistic spirit', whose philosophical foundation had been laid by Islām long before, that can be considered as a continuation of the process of islamization. However, the rationalistic spirit initiated by Islām, if allowed to proceed along its present westernized course, will undoubtedly be deviated in its vision towards secular ends. But the process of islamization is still going on (al-Attas, *ibid.*, p. 2), and the sense in which "Islām had prepared the Archipelago for the modern world to come" was obviously meant to denote not the secularized world, but the islamized world. A truly islamized world is a world disenchanted or deprived first of its magical, mythological, animistic, national and cultural tradition opposed to Islām and then its secular meaning; a world in which political power and authority — other than that of God and His Prophet and of those who follow His Prophet — has been desacralized; a world in which all values — other than those of Islām and the truth as partially found in the great world religious and the good in man and his society according to Islām — have been deconsecrated; a world whose meaning was seen and known and experienced and made conscious of in the time of the Holy Prophet (may God bless and give him Peace!) and his Noble Companions (may God be well pleased with them all!).

والله اعلم بالصواب والحمد لله رب العالمين

والصلاة والسلام على اشرف الانبياء والمرسلين

وعلى اله واصحبه والتا بعين لهم باحسان

الى يوم الدين

General Index and Index of Proper Names

Prepared By
Muḥammad Zainīy ʿUthmān
Research Fellow
(ISTAC)

General Index

and the *sharī'ah* 145
fiqh 170
fiṭrah (original state) 45
   natural state of being 61
   as *dīn* 62,139
freedom
   the power of the rational
      soul to do justice to itself
      141, also *quwwah* and *wus'*
   see also justice
al-funūn (arts or sciences) 144

Germanic 134
Glad Tidings (Gospel) 28, 40
Gordian Knot 12
Graeco-Roman 16, 29, 176
   and Western worldview 105
   languages 177
Greece 134
Greek
   philosophy 22, 33, 179
   cosmology 33, 34
'growing up' 5

habeas corpus 77 n. 82
ḥadd (definition) 144
ḥadīth 143,150
ḥāl (spiritual mood) 71 n. 76
   pl. *aḥwāl* (spiritual states)
ḥanīfan 64
   see also *dīn al-qayyim*
happiness 75
   is knowledge identified with
   justice 142 n. 118
   see also certainty
hawā (natural desire) 155
al-ḥayāt al-dunyā (the life of the
   world) 41, 42
Hebrew 16, 21

Hellenic
   epistemology 6
   thought 12
Hijrah 143
ḥikmah (wisdom) 79, 122, 143,
   145
   and Islamic system of education 160
   God-given knowledge 149
   as core knowledge 163
ḥīsab al-ṣaḥīḥ 60 n. 57
historical relativism 17
   see also secularization
ḥuṣūl (arrival in the soul of the
   meaning of a thing) 171
hudā (Guidance) 140

'ibādah (service)
   and *'amal* 141
   and *iḥsān* 121
   and spiritual knowledge 145
   pl. *'ibādāt* 61, 70, 72 n. 77, 79
   identified with *ma'rifah* 146
   leads to *ma'rifah* 71, see also
      ma'rifah
   man's purpose 139
   service and devotion 67
   constant recitation, reflec-
      tion and contemplation 90
idānah (conviction) 52
iḥsān (perfection in virtue) 67
   n. 68
   also 'The Way' 67 n. 68
   and knowledge 146
   and *sharī'ah* 122, 162
   degrees of 145
   excellence in religious con-
      duct 141
   highest virtue 80
   in the *'abd* 121

191

www.ingramcontent.com/pod-product-compliance
Lightning Source LLC
LaVergne TN
LVHW010513200726
843506LV00013B/2586